INDUSTRIAL TRIBUNALS

EMPLOYMENT LAW GUIDES

PRACTICAL GUIDES TO LAW AT WORK

Other titles in the series:

A Guide to the Employment Acts
Joan Henderson

Handling Redundancy
Sue Morris

Statutory Maternity Pay and Maternity Rights
Gillian Howard (revised by Sue Morris)

Statutory Sick Pay
Gillian Howard (revised by Sue Morris)

Unfair Dismissal – Your Legal Rights
Richard W Painter

*The Work Environment – The Law of Health,
Safety and Welfare*
Patricia Leighton

THE INDUSTRIAL SOCIETY

The Industrial Society is an independent, self-financing organisation with charitable status.

The Society works to develop the full talents and potential of people at work, and those seeking work, and to increase employee involvement and personal fulfilment through work.

The Industrial Society meets these objectives by identifying good practice at work and successful new approaches. These are promoted through courses and conferences, advice, training, information and publications. The Society works in all sectors to guide people towards finding practical solutions which will achieve results in their organisation.

INDUSTRIAL TRIBUNALS

HOW TO PRESENT YOUR CASE

PHILIP PARRY

First published 1991 by
The Industrial Society Press
Robert Hyde House
48 Bryanston Square
London W1H 7LN
Telephone: 071 262 2401

© Philip Parry 1991

ACKNOWLEDGEMENT

The publisher would like to thank the Controller of HMSO for permission to reproduce forms IT1 and IT3 in Appendix 1. These forms are Crown copyright.

British Library cataloguing-in-publication data
Parry, Philip
 Industrial tribunals – how to present your case.
 (Employment law guides)
 I. Title II. Series
 344.42

ISBN 0 85290 918 7

Cover design by Oliver Relfe

Typeset by Acûté, Stroud, Glos.
Printed by The Lavenham Press Limited

CONTENTS

TABLE OF STATUTES

Employment Acts 1980, 1988, 1989, 1990

Employment Protection Act 1975

Employment Protection (Consolidation) Act 1978

Equal Pay Act 1970

Health and Safety at Work Act 1974

Interpretation Act 1978

Industrial Training Act 1965

Race Relations Act 1976

Sex Discrimination Act 1975

Wages Act 1986

TABLE OF STATUTORY INSTRUMENTS

Employment Protection (Recoupment of Unemployment Benefit and Supplementary Benefit) Regulations 1977 (SI 1977 No 674)

Industrial Tribunals (Rules of Procedure) Regulations 1985 (SI 1985 No 16)

Industrial Tribunals (Interest) Order 1990 (SI 1990 No 479)

Race Relations (Questions and Replies) Order 1977 (SI 1977 No 842)

Safety Representatives and Safety Committee Regulations 1977

Sex Discrimination (Questions and Replies) Order 1975 (SI 1975 No 2048)

Transfer of Undertakings (Protection of Employment) Regulations 1981 (SI 1981 No 1794)

TABLE OF CASES

LIST OF ABBREVIATIONS

ACAS	Advisory Conciliation and Arbitration Service
COIT	Central Office of Industrial Tribunals
CRE	Commission for Racial Equality
DE	Department of Employment
EAT	Employment Appeal Tribunal
EPCA 1978	Employment Protection (Consolidation) Act 1978
EOC	Equal Opportunities Commission
ICR	Industrial Cases Reports
IRLIB	Industrial Relations Legal Information Bulletin
IRLR	Industrial Relations Law Reports
IT	Industrial tribunal
IT1	Application to an industrial tribunal
IT3	Notice of appearance by respondent
PHA	Pre-hearing assessment
r	A particular rule of the Industrial Tribunals (Rules of Procedure) Regulations 1985 (SI 1985 No 16)
sch	Schedule to Act of Parliament
s	Section of Act of Parliament

PREFACE

This book is intended to be a practical guide for those who find themselves involved in a legal case involving a dispute at work which arose in England, Wales or Scotland. The law stated is applicable to all three countries unless specified otherwise. It contains information which will help you decide:

- whether you are eligible to make a claim
- whether you should defend the claim or negotiate a settlement
- how to present and argue your case at the tribunal.

Those who need to explore legal points in more detail are recommended to consult one of the books written specifically for lawyers or those who appear regularly before industrial tribunals, such as *Industrial Tribunals: Practice and Procedure*, by M J Goodman,' (Sweet & Maxwell, 1987 (4th edition)), *Industrial Tribunal Practice*, by J Bowers, (Longman, 1987), or *Tribunal Practice and Procedure*, Incomes Data Services (IDS, 1989).

These books are also useful if your problem concerns one of the more specialised jurisdictions of the tribunals such as employers' appeals under the Health and Safety At Work Act 1974 or employees' applications for interim relief under the Employment Protection (Consolidation) Act 1978. In this book I have concentrated on those areas which account for most of the tribunal's case load, such as dismissal, redundancy, discrimination and deductions from wages.

All references to 'the Rules' are to the Industrial Tribunals (Rules of Procedure) Regulations 1985.

1 INTRODUCTION

The origins of the industrial tribunal system

Since the 1960s the world of employment has increasingly been subject to legal rules and procedures. It is one thing for employers and employees to have legal rights and obligations, but it is often another matter altogether when it comes to enforcing those rights in a way which accords with popular notions of 'justice'. It was felt by the Franks Committee on Administrative Tribunals (1957) that, compared with ordinary courts, tribunals offered 'cheapness, accessibility, freedom from technicality, expedition and expert knowledge of a particular subject'.

By and large these advantages do exist in practice and offer both sides involved in disputes at the workplace a practical forum in which to have their problem settled.

The tribunal system was established by the Industrial Training Act 1964 to hear appeals against industrial training levies. Since then the list of legal disputes with which industrial tribunals deal has expanded greatly, as Parliament has come to recognise that they are the most appropriate forum to deal with most employment problems. The tribunal system is headed by a President appointed by the Lord Chancellor, who is in overall charge of the Central Office of Industrial Tribunals (COIT) and the 15 Regional Offices in England and Wales. Each region has a regional Chair and there are about 64 full-time and 100 part-time Chairs scattered throughout England and Wales.

The members of the industrial tribunal

Your case will be heard by a tribunal of three members (by law it can be two with the consent of the parties, but this rarely occurs), each of whom has one equal vote. The case is decided on a majority vote basis (although in the vast majority of cases the decision is unanimous).

The Chair will be a lawyer of at least seven years' standing and sits between two non-lawyer (lay) members who are appointed by the Secretary of State for Employment. One of the members will have been appointed from a panel of employees' representatives (nominated by the TUC and some other specific trade unions), and the other from a panel of employers' representatives (nominated by the CBI and some other specific employers' organisations). It is important to remember that these lay members are present specifically to bring to bear to the decision making process their knowledge of the world of employment and industrial relations. They can, and frequently do, ask expert and penetrating questions of the parties to the case and usually have a well-informed view as to good industrial practice.

In sex discrimination cases the tribunal administration usually tries to ensure that at least one woman member is sitting, and in race relations cases at least one member should have experience of race relations matters (although this does not necessarily mean that they will come from a particular ethnic minority group). It is disappointing to note that despite efforts on the part of the Secretary of State for Employment to increase the proportions of women and ethnic minority members, the number of women members stands at 22 per cent and those from ethnic minorities at 2.7 per cent (*Employment Gazette*, 1990 p219).

While the members are appointed from the panels of both employees' and employers' representatives, they are each expected to be impartial and to decide the case in accordance with the law. Indeed, you might find it impossible to discover from the questions they ask which members come from which panel.

The proceedings are controlled by the Chair who will be concerned to ensure that the case is conducted in an orderly manner, that the rules of evidence are followed and, particularly where one of the parties is unrepresented by a skilled advocate, that the main strengths of each party's case have been produced in evidence.

Rule 8 of the 1985 Regulations provides that the tribunal should conduct the hearing 'in such a manner as it considers most suitable to the clarification of the issues before it', and shall 'so far as appears to it appropriate seek to avoid formality'.

The Chair decides all questions of law which arise during the case. In practice this means that he or she is able to exercise considerable discretion as to how the proceedings will be conducted. Their approach to the case can be very important, particularly in relation to the way they attempt to put witnesses at their ease, and the extent to which they adhere, or otherwise, to the strict rules of evidence (tribunals are not bound by the same rules which apply in ordinary courts of law).

The tribunal also has a clerk whose job is to look after administrative matters relating to the case, such as administering the oaths to witnesses, recording exhibits presented to the tribunal and frequently offering advice to both parties. This advice is often given in the corridor outside the hearing rooms before the case begins or during breaks in the proceedings. Although many of the clerks have considerable experience in employment disputes, it should always be remembered that they are not legally qualified. Therefore, you should hesitate before seeking their advice on either any purely legal point, or whether they think you are going to win or lose the case.

The tribunal's workload

Tribunals are located in 20 centres in England and Wales and four in Scotland, and about 50 tribunals sit at any one time. They deal with an immense case load. If a tribunal centre is particularly busy, cases are sometimes moved to a centre with a lesser case load. Tribunals sit on most days and hear a wide variety of cases, often more than one in a day. In the last year for which statistics are available, 1989–90, there were 31,900 applications registered with the Central Office, of which 57 per cent (18,100) were unfair dismissal claims. Complaints about unlawful deductions from wages accounted for 15.3 per cent of all cases and the remaining percentage was concerned with such diverse matters as race and sex discrimination, redundancy payments and equal pay claims (*Employment Gazette,* 1991 p305).

2 APPLYING TO AN INDUSTRIAL TRIBUNAL

This chapter will allow you to determine whether or not you are entitled to take your complaint to an industrial tribunal, and, if you are, how to go about it. Citizens' Advice Bureaux and law centres can also advise you.

The type of complaints industrial tribunals are entitled to hear and the concept of continuous service

The first point to note is that tribunals cannot hear any complaint relating to a dispute at work unless a particular Act of Parliament has expressly given it authority to do so. At the time of writing, they deal mainly with the types of complaint listed in table 1.

Table 1 – the jurisdiction of industrial tribunals

Type of action	Statutory authority
dismissal:	
complaints	EPCA 1978 s54
written reasons for dismissal	EPCA 1978 s53
pregnancy	EPCA 1978 s60
trade union membership	EPCA 1978 s58
equal pay claims	Equal Pay Act 1970
guaranteed week payment	EPCA 1978 s12
health and safety, appeals by employers	Health and Safety At Work Act 1974

safety representatives and safety committees	Safety Representatives and Safety Committee Regulations 1977
pay statements	EPCA 1978 s8
pregnancy, failure to permit return to work after	EPCA 1978 s45
race discrimination	Race Relations Act 1976
redundancy, consultation	Employment Protection Act 1975 s99
redundancy, payments	EPCA 1978 s81
sex discrimination	Sex Discrimination Act 1975
suspension on medical grounds	EPCA 1978 s19
takeovers and mergers	Transfer of Undertakings (Protection of Employment) Regulations 1981

time off work for:
  ante-natal care
  public duties
  safety representatives
  redundancy
  trade union duties and
    activities
	
	EPCA 1978 s31(A)
	EPCA 1978 s29
	(see health and safety)
	EPCA 1978 s31
	EPCA 1978 s27–8

trade unions:
  exclusion and expulsion
  refused job because of
    membership/
    non-membership
	
	Employment Act 1980 s4
	
	Employment Act 1990 s1 and 2

unjustifiable discipline by a trade union	Employment Act 1988 s3
victimisation	EPCA 1978 s23
wage deductions	Wages Act 1986 s5
written statement of terms and conditions of employment	EPCA 1978 s11

Of particular interest is the fact that the tribunals do not have the authority to hear claims for damages for personal injuries or diseases which arise from work. Nor can they hear claims where compensation is sought for breach of contract or for 'wrongful dismissal', that is, where the applicant claims that he or she was not given the notice, or money in lieu of notice, to which they were contractually entitled. These sorts of claims have to be heard in the High Court or county courts.

In March 1990 the Government announced in Parliament that it intends 'as soon as practicable', to put s131 of the EPCA 1978 into effect. This will mean that employees making a complaint of unfair dismissal at a tribunal will, at the same time, be able to ask the tribunal to award, for example, arrears of lost pay because they were dismissed without any notice (whereas at the moment they would have to go to a tribunal to claim unfair dismissal and then to the county court or High Court to claim for the wrongful dismissal — a patently absurd situation). While this will be a significant improvement over the present position it should be noted that such a claim for breach of contract or wrongful dismissal will probably only be able to be added-on to a claim which the tribunal is already authorised to hear, eg an unfair dismissal or other employment protection claim. It cannot be brought independently and in its own right.

The next consideration is whether you have, or had, enough 'continuous service' with the employer to be entitled to bring a claim. The minimum continuous service requirements vary with the type of complaint being made, and are listed in table 2.

Table 2 — minimum continuous service requirements

Type of action	Requirement
dismissal, complaint (not if reason was sex or race)	2 years (none if reason for dismissal related to trade union membership)
dismissal, written reason for dismissal	2 years
equal pay	none
guaranteed week payment	1 month
maternity dismissal	2 years (none if sex discrimination)
maternity pay	6 months prior to the 14th week before the expected week of confinement
pay statement	none
pregnancy, right to return to work after	2 years at the beginning of the 11th week before the expected date of confinement
race discrimination	none
redundancy, consultation	none
redundancy, payment	2 years
sex discrimination	none
suspension on medical grounds	1 month

takeovers and mergers	none
time off work:	
ante-natal care	none
public duties	none
safety representatives	none
redundancy	2 years at the date when the notice expired
trade union duties & activities	none
trade unions:	
exclusion & expulsion	none
unjustifiable discipline by a trade union	none
victimisation	none
wage deductions	none
written statement of terms and conditions	3 months

'Continuous service' is important not only in establishing whether the applicant is entitled to bring a claim but is often a factor in determining the amount of compensation which tribunals award successful applicants.

A study conducted by Warwick University which was published in 1985 showed that only 12 per cent of employees challenge their dismissals. However, 27 per cent of the applicants were dismissed within the first year of their employment and a further 35 per cent were dismissed between the first and third years of their employment, hence they were unable to succeed in their claims. These statistics clearly demonstrate the importance of all the parties considering this preliminary matter of continuous service (*Dismissal: A Study of Unfair Dismissal and the Industrial Tribunal System* by L Dickens et al, Blackwell).

The rules for computing continuity of employment are complex and are found in schedule 13 EPCA 1978. The length of continuous service should be stated in the written statement of particulars which s1 EPCA 1978 requires employers to supply to employees within

13 weeks of starting work.

The basic rules are as follows:

- an employee's employment is presumed to have been continuous unless the contrary is proved (paragraph 1 (3) of schedule 13)

- normal working weeks: a week counts towards continuous service if the employee actually worked for 16 hours or more (paragraph 3) or was employed under a contract of employment for 16 hours or more, whether or not he or she actually worked these hours (paragraph 4). Alternatively, employees are protected if they worked under a contract which provided for eight hours of work each week and they had worked for the employer for more than five years (paragraph 6). Where a contract which provides for 16 hours or more per week is reduced to less than 16 but more than eight hours, up to 26 weeks at the reduced hours will count (paragraph 7)

- periods in which there is no contract of employment: paragraph 9 provides that a week shall count towards continuity if the employee:

  - was incapable of work in consequence of sickness or injury (a maximum of 26 consecutive weeks is allowed)

  - was absent from work on account of a 'temporary cessation of work'. In *Ford* v *Warwickshire County Council*, Mrs Ford had been employed as a lecturer between 1971 and 1979 on a series of fixed-term contracts which commenced in September of each year and terminated the following July. Her claim for unfair dismissal and redundancy compensation was contested by the employer on the preliminary point that her continous service was less than one year. The House of Lords held that a 'temporary cessation of work' meant 'a relatively short time' in relation to the normal periods of working and that this was a question of fact for the industrial tribunal to decide. It concluded that the break for the summer vacation was capable of being interpreted as temporary and thus remitted her case back to the tribunal which went on to award her a redundancy payment.

  - was absent from work in circumstances such that by arrangement or custom. Examples would include an employee who has been loaned to another employer or an employee given leave of absence for personal reasons such as an extended foreign vacation

- strikes or lock-outs: any week (or part thereof) during which the employee is on strike or has been locked-out by the employer does not count towards the total length of continuous service. However, it does not break it either (paragraph 15)

- change of employer: normally continuity is broken when an employee leaves one employer and starts working for another, but there are exceptions to this rule and hence continuous service is preserved where:

  - there is a transfer of the business (or a part of it) for whom the employee worked and which comes within paragraph 17 (2). The important question is whether there has been a transfer of a 'going concern' (in which case continuity is preserved) or whether the sale was merely of some of the assets of the business (in which case it is not). Industrial tribunals frequently decide this question by examining whether or not there was a sale of the goodwill (which is evidence that the business was sold as a going concern)

  - employment with one body corporate is substituted for another body corporate by an Act of Parliament (paragraph 17 (3))

  - the employee is taken into the employment of an 'associated employer' of the original employer (paragraph 18). This is defined by EPCA 1978 s153(4): 'any two employers are to be treated as associated if one is a company of which the other (directly or indirectly) has control, or if both are companies of which a third person (directly or indirectly) has control'

  - the employer dies and his or her personal representative or trustees keep on the employee (paragraph 17(4))

  - there is a change in the partners, personal representatives or trustees who employ the employee (paragraph 17(5))

— the business is transferred and it comes within the ambit of the (very complicated) Transfer of Undertakings (Protection of Employment) Regulations 1981. However, for the Regulations to apply, that which is transferred must be a commercial venture. If a question arises relating to these Regulations reference should be made to a specialised text such as *Business Transfers and Employment Law: A Practical Guide* by F Younson, (Sweet and Maxwell, 1989).

Those entitled to bring claims and those entitled to defend them

The person bringing the case is known as the applicant or complainant and, as will be seen, he or she does this by sending an application to the Central Office of Industrial Tribunals. The person or organisation against whom the case is brought is known as the respondent, ie the party which responds to the application or complaint which has been made. Usually, the applicant is an employee (eg in a claim involving alleged unlawful deductions from wages), an ex-employee (eg in a case alleging unfair dismissal), or a potential employee (eg where an unsuccessful applicant for a job alleges unlawful race or sex discrimination). Occasionally, however, the employer can be the applicant or complainant, eg where an employer appeals against the issuing of a non-discrimination notice in cases of race or sex discrimination, or against the issuing of an improvement or prohibition notice in health and safety cases.

Applicants frequently make mistakes as to the identity of the respondent, eg name the wrong company or use the name of one of the directors or managers instead of the company name. Such mistakes may be pointed out by either the respondent or the tribunal itself when the relevant forms are received. Mistakes are not necessarily fatal to the claim and the respondent's correct identity can be inserted by the tribunal at the hearing with the consent of the parties. Even if the respondent does not consent, the tribunal can still substitute the correct name, provided it is satisfied that no injustice will occur as a result of it so doing, eg having caused real confusion as to precisely whom the action was being brought against.

The tribunal may, either on its own motion or at the request of one of the parties, add another party as a respondent to the proceedings or delete from the case one of the respondents if it considers that they are no longer directly interested in the matter. It reaches this decision from the information received on the IT3 form. If there are 'numerous persons having the same interest' in an application, one or more respondents may be authorised by the tribunal before or at the hearing to defend the case on behalf of the others (r14).

If there are several cases pending before a tribunal which have similar questions of law or facts, then it is open to the tribunal to order, or any of the parties to request, the proceedings be consolidated into one hearing (r15). For example, a convenient way in which a tribunal can deal with large numbers of equal pay applications, each of which relates to the same employer, is through the selection of sample cases. This avoids the need to hold separate hearings on each individual claim. Before doing this, however, it must give all the parties the chance to object to such a proposal.

In an important case in 1990 the Court of Appeal decided that where there are a large number of cases pending, all of which involve similar factual issues, a tribunal is entitled to hear representative cases and, if these are unsuccessful, dismiss the others (*Ashmore* v *British Coal Corporation*).

In this case, Mrs Ashmore was one of 1,500 employees who worked in the canteen of British Coal. These employees claimed equal pay with a male comparator. The tribunal ordered that all cases, other than 14 sample cases, be stayed. Eventually these claims were dismissed by the EAT. After the appeal, the applicant attempted to have the stay on her claim removed and the case listed for hearing. The tribunal, the EAT and the Court of Appeal dismissed her appeal against this decision, with costs, on the grounds that it was 'vexatious'.

One of the parties or the tribunal itself can direct that somebody else be joined as a party to the proceedings. For example, if an employee was dismissed by the employer for leaving or having been expelled from a trade union in a closed shop situation then the employee, the employer or the tribunal might require the party who had applied industrial pressure to be joined, so there would now be two respondents rather than just the original employer (here it would probably be the trade union). If the applicant's case is successful, the tribunal may order the joined party to pay some or all of the compensation.

Sometimes official bodies with no direct connection to either of the parties are sent details of the case by the tribunal. In all equal pay and sex discrimination cases, for example, the Equal Opportunities Commission is automatically sent full details, as is the Commission for Racial Equality in race discrimination cases (r17(9)).

In the event of either of the parties dying at some point in the proceedings from the submission of the IT1 onwards, the EPCA 1978 s150 and sch 12, provides that the executors or administrators of the estate can carry on the proceedings and any compensation awarded by the tribunal would be payable to such a person. If there has not been a grant of probate or letters of administration have not been taken out, the tribunal can appoint a person to continue in the case, if they were authorised by the deceased before his or her death to act in the proceedings or if they are the widower, widow, child, father, mother, brother or sister of the deceased. The award is made in favour of the dead person's estate.

The time limits for bringing complaints

Having established that the tribunal has the authority to hear your complaint, the next step is to ensure that your complaint is lodged within the time limit laid down by the particular statutory provision. These vary from statute to statute, and are currently those detailed in table 3.

Table 3 – the time limits for bringing complaints

Type of action	Time limit
dismissal:	
complaint	3 months after the effective date of termination
written reason for	3 months after the effective date of termination
equal pay	6 months after the effective date of termination
guaranteed week payment	3 months after the date for which the payment was owed
pay statement	3 months after the effective date of termination
pregnancy, right to return to work after	3 months (or 6 months if redundant) after the effective date of termination
race discrimination	3 months from the date of the discriminatory act
redundancy:	
consultation	3 months after the effective date of termination
payment	6 months after the effective date of termination (The tribunal retains a *discretion* to hear the complaint for up to 6 months after this date)
sex discrimination	3 months from the date of the discriminatory act
suspension on medical grounds	3 months after the effective date of termination

takeovers and mergers	3 months after the effective date of termination
time off work:	
ante-natal care	3 months after day of appointment
public duties	3 months after failure to permit
safety representatives	3 months after failure to permit or pay
redundancy	3 months after failure to permit or pay
trade union duties and activities	3 months after failure to permit or pay
trade unions:	
exclusion and expulsion	6 months from the date of the exclusion or expulsion
unjustifiable discipline	3 months from date of disciplinary action
victimisation	3 months from the date of the act complained of
wage deductions	3 months from when deduction made
written statement of terms & conditions of employment	during the employment or within 3 months after the effective date of termination

It is very important that these time limits are complied with.

Extending the time limits for bringing complaints

In certain limited circumstances the tribunal can extend the time limit for bringing complaints. The main ground upon which it may do this is if the applicant can persuade the tribunal that 'it was not reasonably practicable for the complaint to be presented before the end of the specified period' (EPCA 1978 s67(2)) in the case of unfair dismissal).

In this situation the tribunal can extend the time limit to what it considers to be a reasonable period. Unless the tribunal thinks the case comes within this exception, it cannot waive the time limit, even if the respondent is willing to overlook the matter. It should also be noted that this is considered to be a point of fact and hence would not normally be appealable. For a further explanation of what is considered a point of fact, see page 67.

There have been many cases on this 'not reasonably practicable' point, some of which appear to contradict each other. The leading Court of Appeal case is *Walls Meat Co Ltd* v *Khan*.

This case suggests that it is not reasonably practicable to present a claim in time 'if there is some impediment which reasonably prevents, or interferes with, or inhibits' the presentation of that complaint. Mr Khan was dismissed in July 1976 and a question arose about his entitlement to unemployment pay; proceedings were started to have his case heard by a local tribunal under the National Insurance Acts. Mr Khan knew of his right to claim unfair dismissal and knew that the claim had to be presented within three months, but he wrongly assumed that his case was being dealt with. It was not until December 1976 when the local tribunal gave its decision that he realised that his complaint of unfair dismissal was not being heard by them. He then went to a solicitor and the completed IT1 was received by the COIT on 10 January 1977.

The industrial tribunal held that in these circumstances it was not reasonably practicable for Mr Khan to have presented his complaint within the three month limit and that he had presented it within a reasonable further period. The Court of Appeal dismissed the employer's appeal and supported the finding of the tribunal.

Other examples of where it is not reasonably practicable to present a claim in time would be the illness of the applicant, absence abroad or a postal strike. Another possible example might be a person's complete ignorance of the legal right to lodge a complaint, although given the widespread publicity in recent years of, for example, unfair dismissal laws, this is becoming increasingly difficult to argue. Ignorance of the time limits themselves on the part of the applicant's advisers will not of itself be a ground for an extension of the time limit. Here there would be a need for additional evidence, such as the discovery of crucial new evidence which only led to the appreciation of a legal right from the date of its discovery.

In *James Cook Ltd* v *Tipper*, for example, employees were made redundant but did not submit an IT1 because they believed that work would pick up again. The Court of Appeal held that it was open to a tribunal to find that it was not reasonably practicable for the employees to present their applications until after the ship yard closed down and they realised that their dismissals were final and irrevocable.

Applicants should also note Lord Denning's comment in the Court of Appeal case of *Dedman* v *British Building & Engineering Appliances Ltd*:

> 'if a man engages skilled advisers to act for him − and they mistake the time limit and present the claims too late − he is out. His remedy is against them'.

In this case, 'skilled adviser' included a solicitor, but in subsequent cases the concept has been extended to include a trade union official and a Citizens' Advice Bureau representative.

If the reason for the delay is that the applicant was awaiting the outcome of an internal disciplinary procedure, or the outcome of a criminal trial, this will not of itself be a sufficient ground for an extension of the time limit unless there is some additional factor upon which the tribunal could rely, eg that the applicant had been requested by the employer to delay making the application until the outcome of the internal appeal had been determined, as in *Owen* v *Crown House Engineering Ltd*. In these situations the correct procedure is to apply within the time limit seeking a stay in the proceedings until the outcome of the internal hearing or court case has been determined.

If the applicant succeeds in convincing the tribunal that it was not reasonably practicable to present the claim within the time limit, he or she must still convince it that, having discovered the importance of applying quickly, this was done within a reasonable period. This can often mean that, once it has been brought to the applicant's attention that there are time limits, the application should be lodged within a couple of weeks from when it became reasonably practicable to do so.

How to apply to an industrial tribunal

The claim must be received by the Central Office of Industrial Tribunals within the specified time limit. The vast majority of people who apply (henceforth called 'applicants') do so by completing a form IT1 which can be obtained free of charge from most job centres, Department of Employment Offices, Citizens' Advice Bureaux, law centres and from industrial tribunal offices themselves. A brief booklet entitled *Industrial Tribunal Procedure* should accompany the form.

However, it is not strictly necessary to apply by completing the IT1, as the main legal rules which govern industrial tribunal procedure, the Industrial Tribunals (Rules of Procedure) Regulations 1985 specify, in r1(1), that a valid application is made providing the following written details are supplied to the Central Office:

- the name and address of the applicant
- the name and address of the person against whom the claim is made
- the grounds, 'with particulars thereof', on which the claim is made.

Hence, a letter to the COIT which contained this information would be perfectly valid, but for the sake of convenience applicants are advised to submit an IT1. Tribunals tend to adopt a fairly flexible approach to the form of application and are often prepared to allow applicants to amend the IT1 later in the proceedings provided it does not cause injustice to the other party. For example, incorrect dates of starting or stopping work or details of wages would rarely cause injustice, and hence tribunals would usually allow the correct details to be inserted or amended.

However, if the amended details substantially alter the basis of the claim which the respondent has to meet, the tribunal might feel obliged to grant an adjournment to the respondent in order to prepare what is now a substantially altered case. This sometimes occurs when an unrepresented applicant submits an IT1 and subsequently obtains a representative who wishes to radically alter the application.

A tribunal may also think it appropriate for applicants to supply respondents with further written particulars of the grounds on which their case is based, and of any facts and contentions which are relevant to the case (r4).

If, when an application is received, the Secretary of the Tribunal is of the opinion that it does not seek or, on the facts stated, could not entitle the applicant to a remedy which the tribunal is legally entitled to give, the Secretary can write to the applicant pointing this out. The Secretary might do this, for example, because the applicant has insufficient continuous service to be able to present a claim, or is clearly well outside the statutory time limits for making a claim. Each year usually between 1,200 and 1,500 applications are not registered due to the operation of this rule.

The application will therefore not be registered unless the Secretary receives by way of written reply a request, from the applicant, that the application should be proceeded with (r1(2)). Applicants can still proceed with the case but should bear in mind that should they lose they may be liable for costs.

The best advice to respondents is that if you think that the applicant might be 'time-barred', consider requesting the tribunal to arrange a preliminary hearing which will deal exclusively with this point. This is known as 'asking for directions' from the tribunal (r13(2)). Quite apart from anything else, this will save both parties unnecessary time and expense, and inconvenience to witnesses. Alternatively, you can request a pre-hearing assessment to determine the matter. More information on pre-hearings will be found in chapter 5.

Completing the application form – Form IT1

Many applicants find the IT1 daunting. However, the information sought will probably have to be obtained at some point in time and so the best advice is to gather and marshall it as early as possible. The form is often not as difficult to complete as it might at first appear, particularly if each question is approached in a methodical manner, and ample time is set aside by the applicant and/or their representative.

Applicants should bear in mind the importance of completing the IT1 in a clear, yet succinct manner. The respondent will examine the IT1 carefully to:

1 ascertain the strength of the applicant's case
2 establish contradictions between statements contained in the application and evidence presented at the tribunal hearing

3 consider requesting an adjournment (with the inconvenience to all concerned) if the case presented at the hearing is substantially different from the information contained in the IT1.

The following questions are those to be found on the IT1.

Question 1   Say what type of complaint(s) you want the tribunal to decide

Here the applicant should specify the broad heading which forms the basis of the complaint. It is perfectly acceptable to put a number of headings here if there is doubt as to whether the complaint relates to just one matter. For example, it is acceptable to write:

1 whether I was unfairly dismissed by my employer *and/or*
2 whether I am entitled to be paid a redundancy payment by my employer.

Question 2   Name, address and date of birth of applicant

The first two details are required for obvious reasons. The third is required so that it can be ascertained whether the applicant's age makes him or her ineligible to make a claim, eg over the normal retirement age, and so that redundancy or unfair dismissal compensation can be calculated.

Question 3   Name and address of your representative if you have one

This information is sought so that any further communications from the tribunal covering the case will be sent direct to the representative (usually a lawyer or trade union official) and not the applicant.

Question 4a   Name and address of the employer, person or body (the respondent) you are complaining about

Applicants are sometimes unsure as to the identity of their employer. If there is any doubt then it would be helpful if the names of all reasonably possible employers were put here. It does not matter that several are mentioned and will not make the applicant appear foolish in the minds of the tribunal members.

Question 4b   Give the place where you worked or applied for work, if different from the above

This will normally be the employer's address.

Question 5   What job did you do for the employer (or apply for)? If this does not apply, what was your connection with the employer?

Here the applicant should insert the job he or she actually performed. If this differs from the details contained in the applicant's statement of particulars issued in accordance with s1 EPCA 1978, or contract of employment, make this clear.

Question 6   State the number of normal basic hours you worked each week

Question 7   (a) Basic wages/salary (b) Average take home pay (c) Other bonuses/benefits

The applicant is expected to detail fringe benefits, pension schemes, overtime bonuses, etc.

Question 8   The dates your employment began and ended

Question 9   If your complaint is not about dismissal please give the date when the action you are complaining about took place or the date when you first knew about it

These questions enable all parties to ascertain whether the applicant is qualified to make a claim, eg in a race or sex discrimination case, and/or in the event that they are, to calculate possible compensation.

Question 10   Give the full details of your complaint

The applicant should state here the basic outline of the complaint which the respondent (usually the employer) will be required to refute.
    If insufficient particulars are provided:

- the tribunal has the power to request them, and if they are not forthcoming it can dismiss the application without a hearing ever taking place (r4)

- the respondent may apply for further and better particulars of the applicant's case, and if these are not supplied may apply to the tribunal to have the case dismissed without a hearing (r4).

For more details on seeking further and better particulars of the other side's case, see page 38.

If you wish to state what, in your opinion, was the reason for your dismissal you may do so here, although you may think it futile to engage in guessing games about the respondent's reasons. However, if you are sure of the reason(s) it may help the tribunal members if you state here, briefly, what you think was the principal reason for the dismissal. You will not be compelled to 'stick to' this reason at the actual hearing.

Question 11   For unfair dismissal claimants – which REMEDY would you prefer?

- reinstatement (to carry on working in your old job as before)
- re-engagement (to start another job, or a new contract, with your old employer)

Note: orders for reinstatement or re-engagement normally include an award of compensation for loss of earnings.

- compensation only.

It is perfectly acceptable to ask for all three possible remedies or to place them in order of preference. In any event you can change your mind later, and as the IT1 points out 'the Tribunal will take your preference into account but will not be bound by it'.

What happens once the completed application form is sent to the Central Office of Industrial Tribunals?

Rule 2 of the Industrial Tribunals (Rules of Procedure) Regulations 1985 states that, upon receiving the originating application, the Secretary of Tribunals shall enter the details contained therein on a public document called the Register. If the complaint is within the jurisdiction of the industrial tribunal, satisfies any relevant time limits and qualifying period of continuous employment, it is then sent to the appropriate Regional Office in England or Wales. In Scotland it is held at the Central Office until the notice of appearance has been received before being transferred to the appropriate office. The case is given a reference number (which should be used afterwards in all corre- spondence connected with the case) and a copy of the application is sent to the respondent. The respondent is then provided with infor- mation as to how to 'enter an appearance' (ie to respond to the claim) and the consequences of failing to do so. The Office informs both parties that the services of an ACAS conciliation officer are available to them, and sends a copy of the application to an ACAS conciliation officer. It must be noted that there is no provision for ACAS conciliation in cases concerning redundancy pay, insolvency pay, paid time off for safety representatives, interim relief and written statements of terms of employment.

Lastly, the Regional Office automatically lists the case for hearing before a particular industrial tribunal, usually within 2–6 weeks. The tribunal centre chosen is usually as near the workplace as possible, and although neither applicant nor respondent can select a time, date or place of a tribunal hearing, if they let the tribunal know of dates on which they cannot attend, these will usually be avoided.

The question often arises as to what steps the parties or tribunal must take in order to validly 'deliver' or serve letters or documents to one or the other parties. Rule 17 of the 1985 Rules of Procedure states that valid service of notices may be effected by post or personal delivery to addresses shown on the originating application or notice of appearance or, if no address is shown there, to the last known address or place of business (r17(3)(d)(ii)). The ordinary postal service will suffice unless a second set of documents is being served on a respondent who has failed to 'enter an appearance' or an order has been made requiring the attendance of a witness (r17(5)(a)(b)). In these circumstances the Post Office's recorded delivery service must be used.

In all these cases, unless the contrary is proved, service is deemed to have been effected at the time at which the letter will be delivered in the ordinary course of post (s7 of the Interpretation Act 1978). If the respondent can prove that service did not take place he or she is entitled to a new hearing, if the hearing has already taken place (r10(1)(b)). If one of the parties has no specific address within the UK, the President or Regional Chair has authority to authorise service outside the UK.

If the respondent's address is completely unknown then the President or Regional Chair can authorise what is known as 'substituted service' (r17(6)). This usually means that an advertisement containing details of the application will be inserted into a local newspaper. It is usual for 14 days to be allowed for an answer to this advertisement, which is usually inserted only once. However, any other time limit may be specified. This is counted as valid service of the originating application.

Can I get Legal Aid?

The simple answer to this question is 'no'. This is traditionally said to be because of the costs to the State and because it would introduce undesirable legal formality to the tribunal system.

However, applicants may approach local solicitors under the 'Green Form' scheme and obtain up to £78.50 (£83.50 in London) worth of free legal advice, depending upon their income and capital. The solicitor can give advice but cannot actually represent an applicant at the tribunal. This should enable the solicitor to give general advice concerning the overall merits of the claim, any relevant procedural points and to write letters, make telephone calls and collect evidence, but do note that this is subject to the £78.50/£83.50 limit.

In cases which are particularly complicated, it might be possible for the solicitor to get approval from those who administer the Legal Aid Scheme to obtain a barrister's opinion on a point of law. Otherwise, most trade unions offer advice and representation to their members in what they consider to be appropriate cases (eg those concerned with union membership). Most Citizens' Advice Bureaux and law centres are prepared to offer free advice and sometimes, depending upon their resources, representation to applicants. The Free Representation Unit is also sometimes willing to assist.

It should be noted that law centres, which are funded by the local community, provide a walk in service. They are staffed by both lawyers and lay people, and standards can vary between centres.

In cases involving race and sex discrimination and equal pay, the Commission for Racial Equality or the Equal Opportunities Commission may provide legal advice and representation where they consider that the case raises a point of principle or is so complex that it would be unreasonable to expect an individual to bring the case unaided. If you need help or advice from either Commission, contact them directly.

The Commissioner for the Rights of Trade Union Members is available to assist trade union members who have complaints against their trade unions.

Applicants, respondents and the witnesses of each can claim for certain expenses to be reimbursed by the Department of Employment, eg wages lost as a result of attending the hearing and travelling and subsistence expenses. Legal representatives, trade union officials and employers' association officials are not entitled to claim.

See Appendix 3 for a list of useful addresses.

Should I be legally represented? Who else can argue my case for me?

Given that it was intended that the main attractions of the tribunals were to be 'cheapness, accessibility and freedom from technicality', it would be tempting to say that legal representation is unnecessary and that the parties should take full advantage of r7(6) which allows either party to be represented by virtually anybody of their choice, including friends, relations, employees, trade union officials, etc. Indeed, in many cases trade unions, Citizens' Advice Bureaux and law centres provide representation for applicants of a high and appropriate standard. Similarly, personnel managers and employers' association officials often provide skilled representation for respondents.

Research produced by the Lord Chancellor's Department in 1989 (*The Effectiveness of Representation at Tribunals*) shows that, although representation increases the likelihood of success, many applicants were forced to attend hearings alone because they could not afford legal representation and free representation was either unavailable or limited in scope. The research refuted the argument that simplicity in initiating proceedings and procedural flexibility in hearings rendered representation unnecessary. Specialist representation, it concluded, made a contribution to tribunal decision making. In particular, four problems were highlighted:

- legal complexity of the subject matter
- imperfect understanding of the tribunal's role and powers

- lack of advocacy skills
- general discomfort with the manner in which tribunals conduct cases (eg nervousness caused by the formality of the occasion).

Similarly, research by the Department of Employment (*Employment Gazette*, 1991 p547) shows that about two-fifths of applicants were successful at tribunal hearings. Applicants succeeded in over half the cases when they were represented by a lawyer, compared with under two-fifths when they represented themselves. Respondent employers had a higher success rate when they were represented by their legal or personnel departments, or by an employers' association.

Many tribunal Chairs actively try and assist unrepresented parties, whether they be applicants or respondents. They might do this by suggesting to them questions they should ask of the other side or by asking the questions on their behalf. But practice varies greatly, and at the end of the day the Chair has to tread a thin line between helping one of the parties and appearing to be biased in their favour. This book attempts to address some of the problems faced by unrepresented parties, but you are advised to consider very seriously the advantages to be gained from obtaining skilled representation.

Cases involving alleged race or sex discrimination are often particularly complex. In certain situations – usually where an important point of principle is at stake – the Commission for Racial Equality or the Equal Opportunities Commission may be willing to provide assistance (including the services of lawyers) to applicants (s75 of the Sex Discrimination Act 1975 and s66 of the Race Relations Act 1976). They will assist only actual or prospective applicants. See Appendix 3 for their addresses.

If I lose the case can I be ordered to pay costs?

The losing side is very rarely required to pay the costs of the successful party. Rule 11(1) states that tribunals should not normally award costs except where they think that one of the parties has, in bringing the case in the first place, or the manner in which they conducted it, 'acted frivolously, vexatiously or otherwise unreasonably'. Basically, this means that the conduct must be very bad indeed and costs may be awarded if any of the following occurs:

- the tribunal has been used for an improper purpose, one party knowing full well that there is no substance to the claim and that it is hopeless and doomed to failure. For example, where the case has been brought or defended purely out of spite or to harass the other side
- one party is responsible for completely unnecessary adjournments, eg where vitally important documents are produced for the first time at the hearing which then forces the tribunal to make an adjournment with consequent unnecessary expense and inconvenience to the other side
- there has been a pre-hearing assessment during which the tribunal indicated that one of the parties had 'no reasonable prospect of success' (r6(2))
- the tribunal Secretary indicated upon receipt of the IT1 that the application did not seek, or did not entitle the applicant to a remedy which the tribunal was entitled to award
- applications are withdrawn at the last minute.

For example, in **Wennevold v Shields Instruments**, the applicant brought a 'manifestly groundless' race discrimination case based solely on the grounds that he had one Norwegian parent. The tribunal dismissed the claim as hopeless and awarded £500 costs to the respondent.

In **Brewster v Torch Motor Policies**, the applicant succeeded in her unfair dismissal claim and the tribunal awarded £150 against the employers because they had unreasonably insisted on a pre-hearing assessment when there was obviously a serious claim to be tried.

In two situations costs *must* be awarded. The first is where, without special reason, the respondent has asked for an adjournment to consider the practicability of reinstating an employee when they already knew, at least seven days before the hearing, that this was the wish of the employee. This applies to ordinary unfair dismissal cases. The second situation in which costs must be awarded is where the case involves a failure to allow a woman to return to work after pregnancy (r11(2)).

So, unless you think your case is really weak, do not worry about having to pay costs (in 1989–90 costs were awarded in just 1.8 per cent (185) of cases heard; in 125 of these cases the amount awarded was less than £300 (*Employment Gazette*, 1990 p306)).

The costs and expenses which might be awarded include the travelling and subsistence expenses and lost wages of the successful party and their witnesses, and legal expenses incurred (including the costs of 'in-house' lawyers or employment consultants).

So far as the amount is concerned, the parties can either agree among themselves as to a reasonable amount or the amount may be settled by taxation in the county court if the parties cannot agree. Most often however, the Chair of the Tribunal will establish the amount based on their experience. They have considerable discretion here and the amount often seems to depend upon their assessment of the blameworthiness of the loser and the means of the party against whom costs are awarded. For example, if an applicant is unemployed and living on social security, there will be little point in making a large costs award against them. However, in this case the tribunal might make a token award of perhaps £50–150, as a contribution towards the winner's costs.

It should be noted that it is only the means of the applicant that are considered and not those of a body such as a trade union or the Commission for Racial Equality/Equal Opportunities Commission which may have been supporting or representing the applicant.

To apply for costs you simply make a request for them at the end of the case. Alternatively, you can make written representations to the tribunal within a reasonable time of its conclusion. In Scotland, where the tribunal has made a 'party-and-party' order, the costs ('expenses') are assessed in the Sheriff Court.

3 HOW THE EMPLOYER SHOULD RESPOND WHEN FACED WITH A CLAIM

Should the employer defend?

The first point to note is that defending a claim is likely to cost most employers a considerable amount of money. As will be readily appreciated, while the median award for unfair dismissal compensation is just £1,786, (*Employment Gazette*, 1991 p305) this represents the tip of the iceberg for the employer. If a case is to be defended successfully it is essential that all those involved in the facts of the case are interviewed, probably several times, their actions reviewed, and an assessment made as to the likelihood of success.

In 1988 the Department of Employment published research showing that about one-quarter of employers were simply unable to calculate the costs of the action, while those who did respond estimated the costs to be from £400 in those cases which were withdrawn by the respondent, to about £2,000 for those who lost at the tribunal (*Employment Gazette*, December 1988).

Even if the employer is confident of success, it must also be remembered that costs are only awarded to the successful party if the applicant brought or conducted the case 'frivolously, vexatiously or otherwise unreasonably' (r11(1)). In the unlikely event that costs are awarded, they will certainly not cover the true cost to the employer of defending the case which is that of the large amounts of valuable management time devoted to the case, quite apart from any legal fees which may be payable.

However, the employer may well feel that the cost is a worthwhile price to pay for maintaining the integrity of disciplinary procedures when management have, upon internal investigation, acted correctly, fairly and in accordance with the internal procedure and any relevant

Code of Practice. Regard should also be given to the effect on the business of adverse publicity in the media. Many employers are, for example, increasingly embarrassed at the negative public relations effect of being found by tribunals to have discriminated on racial or sexual grounds.

Conversely, if investigation reveals that the employers have not acted as management thinks in retrospect they ought to have done, then serious thought should be given to settling the case prior to the hearing and remedying the defect which led to the dispute in the first place. It is interesting to note that of all the applications made to tribunals, about 66 per cent of the claims are settled or withdrawn before the hearing. Of the conciliated settlements, the vast majority result in the applicant receiving a sum of money; very few are re-employed. Of the applications that proceed to a full hearing, 39 per cent of the unfair dismissal cases were decided in favour of the applicant in 1989–90 (*Employment Gazette*, 1991 p304). Whichever decision is made, ACAS conciliation should certainly be seriously considered.

Settling the claim using ACAS

ACAS is automatically sent a copy of most IT1s by the COIT (see page 23 for the exceptions). ACAS itself describes the role of the conciliation officer as being to try to help the parties to reach an agreement but not to act as an arbitrator as to the merits of the case, nor to impose a particular settlement. How the role is fulfilled depends very much on the individual officer. This sometimes involves face-to-face discussions with both sides individually, sometimes meeting them together, but perhaps most often telephoning each side and ascertaining whether there is sufficient common ground for a settlement. The officer should not advise either party on the merits of the case. His or her aim should be to assist the parties to reach an informed decision as to how best to proceed. This may involve explaining relevant law, tribunal procedure, liability for costs, how tribunals assess compensation and guidance about the drafting of terms of settlement.

Section 134 of the EPCA 1978 states that in dismissal cases the conciliation officer should attempt to promote the re-employment of the employee and, failing this, help both sides agree on an amount of compensation. If the conciliation officer has 'taken action' and succeeds in facilitating a settlement, then s140(2) of the EPCA provides that an employee is thereafter precluded from pursuing the claim before any industrial tribunal. The conciliation officer usually tries to ensure that both sides understand and agree to the terms of the settlement and explains the finality of the agreement, together with the advantages of agreeing to it. He or she then inserts the terms into an official form 'Agreement in Respect of a Request for Conciliation Made to ACAS' (called a COT3) which contains the words 'in full and final settlement of all claims by the applicant against the respondent'. It means, legally, precisely that.

It should be noted that it is only this kind of settlement, involving ACAS, which can preclude the applicant from applying to a tribunal at some future date. Even if an informal settlement (one not involving ACAS) between the parties was expressed 'in full and final settlement' an applicant could still take a case to an industrial tribunal. However, if this did happen, and the applicant succeeded in his or her claim, any money previously paid would be taken into account by the industrial tribunal in assessing compensation.

Sometimes ACAS receives requests for its conciliation services from parties who have not submitted completed IT1 forms and who have no intention of applying to a tribunal. This might occur, for example, where both the employer and the employee have agreed that the latter should leave the organisation on an amicable basis. The parties might then want the agreement made binding by completing the COT3.

However, it should be noted that in 1990 ACAS completed a review of its operations and decided that in the light of its increasing case load and strained financial resources it would reduce its 'non-statutory' work. The result is likely to be that conciliation officers will be unwilling to become involved in cases where neither side is claiming a breach of its statutory employment rights. Whether or not the new policy will discourage voluntary settlements which would formerly have been reached remains to be seen.

Settling the claim at the tribunal hearing

Even if both parties do not agree to an ACAS conciliated settlement this is by no means the end of the story. In practice, settlements are frequently agreed in the waiting rooms or corridors on the day of the tribunal hearing. Indeed, even during the actual hearing of the case the parties themselves often decide to ask for a short adjournment so that they can attempt to settle. The Chairs sometimes suggest to the parties that they should consider going outside the hearing room to try and reach agreement. This might be because the evidence of a witness has come out in a different way to that which was expected, or that an important document, the existence of which one side was previously ignorant, has now been produced.

Another attraction of this kind of settlement is that it can contain terms which are beyond the usual range of remedies tribunals can award. For example, it might provide that the respondent will supply a testimonial to the applicant, that confidentiality relating to certain matters will be maintained or that a sum relating to outstanding holiday or sick pay will be included in the overall amount of compensation.

It should also be noted that this form of compensation will not be subject to the Employment Protection (Recoupment of Unemployment and Supplementary Benefit) Regulations 1977 whereby unemployment and supplementary benefits received by the applicant might have to be paid back. The usual procedure here is to ask the tribunal to make a 'consent order' with the terms agreed either inserted into the order or attached in a separate schedule of agreed terms. A slightly different variation is for the applicant simply to withdraw the originating application and for the tribunal to dismiss the case. With these kind of settlements it is usual to specify 7–14 days as the time given for payment of any money due. If the money is not paid within the specified time, the applicant is free to go back to the tribunal and continue with the case. In these circumstances a hearing will be arranged almost immediately. When the money is paid the applicant should notify the tribunal office and the case is then terminated.

Defending the claim

The first thing to do is to decide whether you will be able to return the completed form IT3 'Notice of Appearance by Respondent' to the tribunal within 14 days of having received it (r3(1)). Tribunals are generous in allowing extensions of time if respondents have any kind of reasonable explanation. Indeed, if they receive no response they will send a reminder asking for one and r3(3) states that when the Notice of Appearance is finally received it shall be deemed to request an application for an extension!

Having said this however, your case and your organisation will appear more polished and professional if it does comply with time limits without having to be sent reminders. Fourteen days is a very short time to complete the forms (particularly if you are consulting outside professional advice) and so a holding letter to the tribunal often makes good sense.

As with IT1s, it is not compulsory to use the IT3 form that will have been sent together with a copy of the employee's originating application, but in practice most respondents find it convenient to use it. It is vitally important to read the applicant's IT1 carefully before completing the IT3. For example:

- Establish the nature of the claim against you (question 1)
- Are the details concerning the respondent accurate? (question 4)
- Are the details concerning the following similarly accurate:
  - the applicant's job? (question 5)
  - the applicant's working hours? (question 6)
  - the applicant's income? (question 7)
  - the applicant's dates of employment? (question 8).

If not, use the IT3 to supply the correct details.

If the IT1 contains insufficient details to defend the claim then consider requesting from the applicant further and better particulars of the IT1. Inform the COIT that you have done this and formally apply for an extension of time in which to 'enter an appearance'.

Filling in the IT3

Question 1   Name and address of respondent

Question 2   Do you intend to resist the application?

If the answer is no, this is the time to agree with the applicant or their representatives an agreed settlement.

Question 3   Was the applicant dismissed?

Question 4   Are the employment dates given by the applicant correct?

Question 5   Name and address of your representative

All further communications will be sent directly to this person or organisation.

Question 6   Are the details supplied by the applicant concerning wages/benefits/other payments correct?

Question 7   (maternity cases only) Did you have more than five employees?

Question 8   Give sufficient details to show the grounds on which you intend to resist the application

This is the most important question.

How much detail should you write down here? On the one hand, if you just baldly state 'it was fair to dismiss this person' or 'misconduct', it is highly likely that you are simply delaying the day when you are forced to supply the details as to why you acted in the way you did. You are likely to lengthen the whole proceedings, make the case and your organisation appear in a poor light and not gain any substantial tactical advantage. On the other hand, if you supply several pages of closely-typed detail which you say justifies your dismissal decision, you will have stated the complete details of your case in advance. This may lead to a number of problems.

First, it may mean that at the hearing you are tied to these statements, despite subsequent developments which may have taken place (eg having taken legal advice) and might not be allowed to significantly alter your case at the hearing.

Second, a tribunal cannot find in favour of an employer for reasons which the employer did not argue or in direct contravention of arguments which were presented to it. This would be likely to prejudice the applicant. It is, however, always possible to request the tribunal to amend the IT3 before the hearing commences. Indeed, such a request can be made during the hearing itself, although the tribunal would be much less likely to accede to the request because it may believe it unfair to the applicant who attended thinking they had to meet one set of arguments only to find that they now have to meet a different set. Perhaps the best the respondent could hope for here would be for the tribunal to grant an adjournment to a future date in order for the applicant to prepare their case anew in return for the employer agreeing to pay any costs incurred as a result.

Third, some of your important evidence (either from a witness or document) might not be as convincing on the day as you anticipated. This may significantly weaken your overall strategy.

In view of these problems, it is perhaps best to write down a list of the facts of the case which you are confident are uncontroversial and which you would be happy to agree as accurate with the applicant. Try to ensure that the reason you give, for example, for the dismissal, agrees with any written reasons you previously supplied to the applicant. You should also ensure that mention is made of any relevant Code of Practice, advisory handbook or disciplinary/grievance procedures to which you had regard when taking the action which is now the subject of complaint. In this way the applicant is likely to be supplied with a fair amount of detail concerning the grounds on which the employer resists the claim.

Remember that it is always possible to plead in the alternative. This allows you to argue your case on a number of different footings, and while the tribunal may find against you on one point it may find in your favour on another. For example, you might plead that the employee was not, in fact, dismissed. In the alternative however, he or she was dismissed for misconduct.

Finally, it should be noted that after having received an application the COIT sends a copy to the respondent and to an ACAS conciliation officer (r3(1)). If the respondent fails to 'enter an appearance' then the case still proceeds with the tribunal using the IT3 as evidence. The respondent is not entitled to take any part in the proceedings, which considerably weakens his or her position.

However, having said this, r3(2) provides that it is always open to respondents to apply for an extension of time for entering an appearance, to request further and better particulars of the applicant, to be sent a copy of the tribunal's decision, to be heard at the assessment of compensation, and to seek a review of that decision if the respondent lost the case.

The respondent cannot therefore ask for witness orders or for discovery of documents, and would not normally be able to make verbal or written representations to the tribunal when it decides the case (unless the tribunal decided to allow this on the grounds that it constituted an application for an extension of time).

4 PREPARING YOUR CASE

Preliminary work you should do prior to the hearing

Many experienced tribunal lawyers maintain that most cases are won or lost, not as a result of brilliant cross-examination, but as a result of careful groundwork prior to the hearing. It is usually helpful to try and establish through correspondence with the other side a list of agreed facts. This narrows the area of dispute so that full attention can be paid to those areas where the parties disagree. This saves time, trouble and often money for all concerned.

Once a list of disputed facts has been established it then becomes necessary to decide upon how best to prove your case. Remember that in civil law cases such as these you must prove your case 'on a balance of probabilities', ie it is more likely than not that the other party broke the law (see pages 51–53 for advice as to upon whom the burden of proof is placed). This might involve you using a combination of:

- further particulars from the other side
- obtaining documents from the other side
- bringing witness(es) to the hearing.

Having decided upon the type of evidence you are going to use at the hearing, the usual practice is simply to ask those with the information or documents to let you have it (or a copy of it), or the witness to attend. Often this presents few difficulties, but in the event of a problem arising, then you are advised to write to the tribunal 'for directions' as to how to proceed on these preliminary points and enclose copies of your original request. The matter is decided by a Chair sitting alone, who may well decide the matter by post, relying on the written representations made by the parties, or who may require the parties to appear before him or her. The test usually adopted is that in one way or another the parties have a right to know the sort of thing which is going to be the subject of the hearing.

Seeking further and better particulars of the other side's case

Rule 4(1) states that any party or the tribunal itself may require the other side to furnish written particulars of the grounds on which they rely and of the facts relevant to those grounds by a specified date.

The most common requests for further particulars concern requests for the details behind vague statements or assertions such as precise job title, job duties, dates, times, places, names, titles of documents, location of machinery, previous warnings, etc. If the applicant specified what he or she thought was the reason for the dismissal in the IT1 the respondent might now ask for further particulars of the allegation. Chairs are conscious of the importance of not over-formalising the proceedings, particularly if they think the particulars sought are burdensome, unnecessary or simply a 'fishing expedition' where the results are unlikely to justify the effort needed to find and produce them. Essentially they ask themselves the question:

> 'Is the person seeking the particulars asking for details of the substance of what is going to be said against them so that when they come to the tribunal they will know the nature of the case they have to deal with and have the appropriate evidence to deal with it?'

Colonial Mutual Life Assurance Co v Clinch

For example, in this case the applicant stated in his IT1 that he had been dismissed for 'redundancy/victimisation'. The respondent employer requested particulars of this statement and for discovery of all documents the applicant intended to rely on relating to the matter. The Chair of the tribunal refused the respondent's request but this decision was overturned on appeal by the EAT on the grounds that the respondent was entitled to know the nature of the case he would have to meet at the tribunal. Here the applicant should provide sufficient particulars so as to enable the respondent to know the substance of the allegations and any documents which were relevant to them.

If the Chair orders the disclosure of particulars but the other side refuses to comply, the penalty can be two-fold:

- a fine of up to £400
- the offending party's case can be dismissed, or part of the case can be dismissed, (after having given the offending party the opportunity to state why this should not be done).

In discrimination cases there is special provision in the relevant legislation whereby the applicant can ask questions of the respondent as to his or her reasons for taking or failing to take action regarding certain events which the applicant believed constituted discrimination (Sex Discrimination (Questions and Replies) Order 1975; Race Relations (Questions and Replies) Order 1977). This procedure can be used before the application is submitted or within 21 days after submission.

The answers received in response to the questions can be presented as evidence at the hearing. This is a very valuable aid to applicants in preparing and proving their case. With a little thought the questions can be very penetrating. Respondent employers are strongly advised to consider their replies carefully and to ensure that their replies are truthful and accurate. If the respondent deliberately fails to reply or is evasive the tribunal may draw any inferences it wishes from this up to and including a finding that the respondent did in fact discriminate.

The forms themselves are widely available from such places as job centres, Department of Employment offices, Citizens' Advice Bureaux, law centres and the CRE and EOC.

Making an application to obtain documents held by the other side

You have the right to 'discover' (in Scotland the term used is 'recover') and take copies of documents held by the other side which you believe are relevant to your case. For example, an applicant might seek to discover a written statement of his or her terms and conditions of employment; company rules and disciplinary procedure; details of written warnings concerning their performance or conduct. An example concerning respondents is *Mayfair Ventilation v Bryant*. In this case, employees were dismissed on the grounds that they had taken part in the activities of a rival company, of which they were directors. The employer successfully applied for discovery of documents relating to the activities, suppliers and customers of the rival company.

Formally, the tribunal has the same powers to order disclosure as those of the county court (r4(1)). In practice this means that the Chair will make an order if he or she believes it to be relevant and necessary for a fair disposal of the case and which will not impose unfair additional costs out of proportion to the usefulness of the documents.

For example, in **British Telecommunications v Matthews**, the applicant claimed she had been victimised by her employer because she had engaged in trade union activities while she was a shop steward. This had manifested itself in a poor annual performance appraisal. She applied for discovery of the appraisal forms of all 70 staff employed at her telephone exchange. The request was granted by the tribunal but modified on appeal to the EAT to cover only the eight other staff who had been appraised by her particular manager.

It is important to remember that neither side is required to volunteer a list of documents in their possession. It is for each side to ask. However, if one party chooses to make a voluntary disclosure of the documents in their possession they must not be unfairly selective in their disclosure. Once a party has disclosed certain documents they are under a duty not to withhold further documents (regardless of whether they support their side of the case or not) if there is any risk that the effect of withholding them might be to convey to the other side, or to the tribunal, a misleading impression as to the true nature or effect of a document which they did disclose.

For example, in **Birds Eye Walls Ltd v Harrison**, the EAT held that the respondent employer was in breach of a duty to disclose. While disclosing a minute of the disciplinary interview which preceded the applicant's dismissal he failed to give discovery of the findings of a working party of senior company executives into alleged malpractices on the part of employees. This report recorded a decision that Mr Harrison be dismissed, which had been taken before the disciplinary interview at which he was ostensibly going to be offered the opportunity of answering the charges against him. The EAT therefore ordered that the case be remitted to the industrial tribunal, with Mr Harrison granted leave to amend his IT1 so as to argue the case on the basis of a breach of the principles of natural justice.

Documents frequently sought include the following:

- written particulars of employment
- letters of engagement

- letters of appointment or promotion
- letters of dismissal
- written warnings
- records of disciplinary hearings
- documents showing mitigation of loss by the applicant (eg details of jobs they have applied for since the dismissal).

In an equal pay claim you might want the employer to disclose the job descriptions of other employees so as to enable you to identify a comparator.

Obtaining documents held by the other side is particularly relevant in discrimination cases and is often the most important evidence in the applicant's case. For example, if an applicant's case is that they were not selected or promoted because of race, they would clearly wish to have such details of the short listed candidates as their qualifications, experience, ethnic origin, age, references, annual reviews, etc and then compare them with their own in order to see if it was possible to draw inferences of discrimination.

The vital role of statistical evidence was highlighted in one of the most important discrimination cases ever to have been decided, *West Midlands Passenger Transport Executive* v *Singh*. Here the Court of Appeal declared that:

'if a practice is being operated against a group then, in the absence of a satisfactory explanation in a particular case, it is reasonable to infer that the complainant, as a member of that group has himself been treated less favourably on grounds of race'.

In this case, Mr Singh obtained voluntary discovery of a schedule showing the ethnic origins, qualifications and experience of all applicants for the post of senior inspector. However, the employers resisted his application for discovery of details of the ethnic origins of applicants for, and appointees to, posts within a band of grades broadly comparable to that for which he had applied. The tribunal made an order for discovery of those details. The Court of Appeal agreed with the tribunal, making the point that evidence that an employer has or has not appointed any or many ethnic minority applicants in the past is material to whether he has discriminated against a particular applicant. Thus applicants to the industrial tribunals are entitled to discovery to ascertain the percentages of successful minority applicants and successful white applicants for comparable jobs.

The Court of Appeal case of **Baker v Cornwall County Council** has clearly established that, once a prima facie case has been made out, the evidential burden shifts to the respondent employer who must provide a clear and specific explanation disproving the inference. What is meant by a prima facie case is evidence from which a tribunal would conclude that there was discrimination if there was no evidence in rebuttal from the respondent employer.

In this case the tribunal found, on the facts, that Mrs Baker had not been discriminated against on the grounds of her sex when she applied for a job as a site surveyor. The Court of Appeal declined to overturn the decision on the grounds that the tribunal had been satisfied with the explanation given to them that the application had been dealt with on its merits and that it would be wrong to interfere with it.

The message from these cases is clear: employers should monitor their employees in accordance with the recommendations of the Commission for Racial Equality and the Equal Opportunities Commission. The recommendations of the former is entitled *Code of Practice for the Elimination of Racial Discrimination and the Promotion of Equality of Opportunity in Employment,* and the latter *Code of Practice for the Elimination of Discrimination on the Grounds of Sex and Marriage and the Promotion of Equality of Opportunity in Employment.* The results of the monitoring exercise are 'discoverable' by applicants. A failure to monitor in accordance with the Code might well lead the tribunal to draw an adverse inference.

In the EAT case of **Carrington v Helix Lighting Ltd**, Mrs Carrington answered an advertisement for light assembly workers. She was interviewed for two to three minutes and was rejected for the job. Advertisements continued to appear in the local newspapers. She brought a case alleging racial discrimination and requested details of the ethnic composition of the company's workforce. The respondent company refused to supply these on the grounds they were simply not available. The tribunal Chair refused the applicant's request on the grounds that the application did not fall within the scope of 'discovery', since discovery relates to existing documents. Nor did the application fall within the category of 'particulars' because these relate to the basis whereby a party ascertains the way the other side is putting their case so that they can prepare accordingly.

However, the EAT was of the opinion that while tribunals cannot order employers to carry out a survey of the ethnic composition of their workforce if they do not have this information, nevertheless the applicant can use the question and answer procedure to obtain the information. A failure to answer the questions properly might well lead the tribunal to draw an adverse inference.

A major House of Lords case, **Science Research Council v Nasse** decided that while employers are perfectly entitled to object to releasing what they believe to be confidential information, there is no absolute rule of law preventing the tribunal awarding disclosure. In this case, Mrs Nasse was Chair of the local branch of her trade union and was not selected to appear before an interview panel, an essential step in the procedure for promotion from clerical officer to executive officer. She claimed that her employer had discriminated against her both on the grounds of her trade union activities and marital status. Her employer voluntarily supplied her with her own annual confidential report but refused to provide those of two of her colleagues who were selected for interview. The Chair of the industrial tribunal granted an order that the documents should be supplied to her, and the House of Lords agreed with this decision.

The situation is, therefore, that in the event of a dispute, the Chair will usually inspect the documents to decide whether it is necessary to release them in the interests of justice and for a fair disposal of the case. Among other considerations it will be taken into account whether the same information could be obtained from alternative, non-confidential sources and this might, and often does, include blanking out the actual names, addresses and telephone numbers of other candidates and substituting letters of the alphabet.

Tribunals encourage open disclosure between the parties on a voluntary basis. This means that each party disclose to the other all relevant documents in their possession. Indeed, both parties will be sent a form requesting that they send to the other side and to the tribunal a list of documents which they intend to produce at the hearing.

However, certain documents are privileged and do not have to be disclosed. Confidentiality has already been dealt with above but in addition, disclosure will not be ordered in the case of documents which are:

- subject to the rules relating to public interest. For example, a government department may successfully argue that disclosure would be contrary to the public interest
- subject to the rules relating to legal privilege. Communications between a party and their adviser/representative which specifically concern the case are privileged, eg lawyers, trade union officials, personnel officers
- communications to an ACAS conciliation officer in connection with the case, unless the party making the statement waives their right to resist disclosure
- communications between the parties in relation to resolving the dispute or for facilitating a settlement. These cannot be 'discovered'.

The consequences of failing to comply, without reasonable excuse, with a tribunal's order for discovery are that the originating application or Notice of Appearance may be 'struck out' in whole or in part, the employer might be prevented from continuing to defend the claim (r4(4)) and the party in default may be fined up to £400.

Bringing witnesses to the hearing

You should think very carefully about compelling witnesses to attend the hearing if they do not wish to do so. The analogy is sometimes drawn with an unexploded bomb – it can go off in your face with little or no warning. However, if you do think that witnesses' evidence is of particular importance and you think they will not attend voluntarily, you can apply in writing to a tribunal Chair to make an order under r4(b)(iii). You should specify in a fair amount of detail why you think the witnesses' evidence is important to your case and why you think they will not attend unless an order is made. This could be because witnesses might wish to safeguard their position in relation to their own employer or could simply be that their employer refuses to release them without an order. Witnesses can also apply to the tribunal to have the order set aside because, for example, their evidence will be of little value.

If the order is deliberately disobeyed then the transgressor may be fined up to £400. This is put in motion when the fact that the order has been disobeyed is brought to the attention of the Chair of the tribunal.

You should think carefully about the number of witnesses you wish to introduce, and ensure that you limit them to the minimum number necessary to present the most relevant parts of your case. If you attempt to produce too many witnesses you may well find the Chair asking you, before they begin their testimony, what relevant evidence the witness is likely to produce.

So far as financial considerations are concerned, the party calling the witness must pay reasonable travelling expenses to the hearing. However, the tribunal clerk will arrange for any loss of earnings and a subsistence allowance (a basic sum paid by the State) to be paid from public funds.

5 PRE-HEARING ASSESSMENTS

What is a pre-hearing assessment?

One or both sides may by now have a good idea of the strengths and weaknesses of the other's case. You may conclude that the other side's case is so weak that you wish the tribunal to hold a pre-hearing assessment in advance of the full hearing so that it can be weeded out. Indeed, the tribunal itself can order that such a procedure be followed (r6(1)). Both sides will be asked to attend what is normally a brief hearing and will be asked to argue their case but not produce any evidence. If the tribunal considers the case 'to have no reasonable prospect of success' it will inform the party accordingly and warn them that if they exercise their right to take the case to a full hearing and lose, they may be liable to pay the costs.

In recent years there has been a sharp decline in the use of pre-hearing assessments. In 1989–90, 545 PHAs were held of which 269 resulted in the applicant receiving a costs warning. The result was that just 42 of those cases (16 per cent) actually went on to a tribunal hearing. In 33 of these cases the applicant lost, but only 12 cost orders were made (*Employment Gazette*, 1991 p306).

The advantages of PHAs to respondents are that hopeless cases can be weeded out at an early stage with consequent savings in time, expense and adverse publicity. The disadvantage is that if the respondent's application is unsuccessful it will have involved at least two hearings with consequent added time and expense. It might also have increased the self-confidence of the applicant by having reached such a stage, and his or her unwillingness to settle (and the price at which they are prepared to settle).

Can I be required to pay a deposit in advance?

The Employment Act 1989 s20 provides that tribunals will be able to hold 'pre-hearing reviews' and, if they consider the case to have 'no reasonable prospect of success', to order either party to pay a deposit of up to £150 as a condition of proceeding further with the case. Presumably, any costs subsequently awarded would be paid from the deposit; if the costs were over £150 the party incurring the costs would pay the balance.

At the time of writing, we await the publication of detailed regulations to govern this procedure. It is interesting to note that this provision has been subject to considerable criticism from a number of bodies (see for example, the 1988–9 annual report of the Council on Tribunals). The criticism rests chiefly on the grounds that its main effect is unlikely to discourage merely hopeless cases, but rather to discourage other applicants, many of whom will have strong cases but who are worried that they will have to pay a deposit which they might not be able to afford.

6 YOUR DAY AT THE TRIBUNAL

Arriving at the tribunal, the timing and length of the hearing

The case is likely to be heard between about 12 and 20 weeks after the application was received by the COIT. In 1990, 50 per cent of applications were heard within 12 weeks of the receipt of the IT1, 70 per cent within 16 weeks and 83 per cent within 20 weeks (*Hansard* 30.11.90). Tribunals normally give at least two weeks' notice of the hearing and often give much longer. You are entitled to ask for an adjournment to a later date but will need a cogent reason which should be supported by evidence of the difficulty giving rise to the application. Personal inconvenience would not normally be sufficient; the outcome of a pending civil or criminal court case, or the illness of a vital witness, might well be.

Cases rarely last for more than one day and hence are normally scheduled by the tribunal staff to last for one day. This means that you should attempt to estimate whether your case is going to go on longer than this. If it is, you are strongly advised to write to the tribunal in advance asking for a specified number of days to be allocated to the case and stating your reasons. If you fail to do this and the case has to be adjourned at the end of the first day there is likely to be a very substantial time delay, with consequent inconvenience to all concerned.

Most tribunals start at 10 am so you should aim to arrive by 9.30 am at the latest and check in with the clerk at the reception desk.

You will be directed to a waiting room reserved exclusively for applicants and their witnesses, or for respondents and their witnesses. This is the time to discuss any procedural problems with the tribunal clerk, reassure your witnesses and, perhaps, consider again the possibility of reaching a settlement. It is at this stage that representatives frequently meet in the corridor and arrive at a settlement.

The clerk will later arrange for you to be escorted into the room where the hearing will take place. You may be surprised at the informality of the room – it will probably look more like a large Civil Service office than a courtroom. Gowns or wigs are not worn but people are neatly dressed. The three members of the tribunal are addressed as 'sir' or 'madam'. Everybody sits at the same level apart from the members who will usually have their desk on a raised platform so that everybody can see them clearly. The Chair will invite the parties to introduce themselves and their representative. The case now commences.

It is the usual practice to stand up when the tribunal members enter or leave the room, but thereafter to remain seated except when in the witness box.

Confidential information will be disclosed – can I request a hearing in private?

Hearings are normally open to members of the press and public (r7(1)). In certain specific circumstances, however, the tribunal can order that the case, or the evidence of a particular witness, be held in private because:

- it is in the interests of national security to so do, *or*
- information may be included which the witness could not disclose without breaking the law, *or*
- information was communicated to the witness in confidence, *or*
- information may be included, the disclosure of which would cause substantial injury to any undertaking (other than in respect of its effect on collective bargaining negotiations).

You will need to argue a very strong case for the tribunal to exercise its powers under r7(1). Although the tribunal can be asked that the case be held in private on the day of the hearing, it is strongly recommended that you notify it in advance.

I want the tribunal to look at some documents – how do I arrange this?

The best advice is to agree in advance with the other party a list of documents which you both want the tribunal to look at, eg the applicant's statement of particulars issued under s1 of the EPCA 1978, a contract of employment issued to the applicant, the respondent's work's rules book and the respondent's disciplinary or grievance procedure. You can arrange this by letter or by telephone. You then both agree on the order in which this bundle of documents will be presented, marking the first No 1, the second No 2, and so on.

If no common system is agreed the applicant should number his or her bundles A1, A2, etc, and the respondent R1, R2, etc. As you will want the tribunal members and the witnesses to have access to a copy, you should ensure that six copies of the documentation are produced. Remember, the fact that you have both agreed to include a particular document in the bundle does not mean that you necessarily agree as to the accuracy of its content.

What happens if one of the parties fails to turn up?

If one of the parties fails to turn up, the tribunal has the discretion to dismiss the case, adjourn it, or treat the IT1 or IT3 as a written representation and proceed with the case (r7(4)). Written representations are statements made to the tribunal by either party. Rule 7(3) states that to qualify they must have been received by the tribunal and the other party at least seven days in advance of the hearing. Representations are usually submitted in this way when one of the parties does not intend to turn up at the hearing.

The importance the tribunal attaches to these representations depends largely upon whether the facts of the case (as opposed to any legal point involved) are agreed by the parties. If the parties disagree as to the facts then representations carry relatively little weight because the absent party is unavailable to be cross-examined on them. Where the facts are agreed representations are obviously much more important. The usual practice, however, when one party fails to appear is for telephone calls to be made to establish their whereabouts. If this is unsuccessful the hearing will be adjourned to a later date.

The procedure at the tribunal and the different stages of the hearing

The tribunal has considerable discretion as to how the case should proceed. All that r8(1) requires is that the tribunal should seek to avoid formality and states that it should not be bound by the strict rules of evidence which govern normal court proceedings. Subject to the other Rules the tribunal may regulate its own procedure (r12). This means that the tribunal has the power to regulate its own procedures and thus retains considerable discretion as to the conduct of the case. Naturally, Chairs vary in the way in which they exercise discretion.

So far as procedure itself is concerned both parties are entitled to give evidence, to call witnesses, to cross-examine witnesses and to address the tribunal (r8(2)). The various different stages of the procedure at the tribunal hearing can be found in table 4 (see pages 52–3).

Who starts the case – the standard of proof and the burden of proof

The party who starts (or 'opens') the case is usually (though by no means always – see r8(1) above) the one who has to discharge the burden of proof. The statute the case is being brought under declares who has to do the 'proving'.

The *standard of proof* required in a tribunal is the same as in the ordinary civil courts, ie the case has to be proved 'on a balance of probabilities.' This is lower than the standard of proof required in the criminal courts which requires the court to be satisfied of the defendant's guilt 'beyond a reasonable doubt'.

The *burden of proof* in tribunals, ie which party has to prove their case on a balance of probabilities, varies according to which statute the claim is being brought under. For example, in unfair dismissal cases:

- the applicant must prove he or she was dismissed, if this is disputed by the respondent employer
- once the dismissal has been agreed or established by the evidence it is for the respondent employer to show the reason for the dismissal
- the burden between the parties is neutral so far as the reasonableness of the dismissal is concerned.

In redundancy payment cases:

- the applicant must prove he or she was dismissed, if this is disputed by the respondent employer
- it is for the respondent employer to prove that the employee was not dismissed by reason of redundancy (because the EPCA 1978 s91(2) presumes the dismissal was by reason of redundancy).

In race and sex discrimination cases:

- it is for the applicant to establish a prima facie case, but once this has been achieved the burden shifts to
- the respondent to establish that his or her actions were not unlawful acts of race or sex discrimination.

In most other cases which come within the jurisdiction of industrial tribunals the burden of proof lies upon the applicant.

Table 4 – the hearing

1 Very occasionally, Chairs in England and Wales will allow an opening statement by the party on whom the burden of proof lies (the first party). It is very rare indeed for this to be allowed in Scotland

2 First party presents their evidence and their witnesses. Each witness:

- will give their evidence-in-chief
- can be cross-examined by the second party
- can be re-examined by the first party

3 Opening statement by the second party. Again, this is only very occasionally allowed in England and Wales, and almost never in Scotland

4 Second party presents their evidence and their witnesses. Each witness:

- will give their evidence-in-chief

- can be cross-examined by the first party
- can be re-examined by the second party

5   Closing address by the second party

6   Closing address by the first party

7   Tribunal makes its decision

The opening statement

Parties no longer have the legal right to make an opening statement and Chairs increasingly discourage such a practice. They prefer the parties to start the case by presenting their evidence (this is particularly so in Scotland). However, both parties and Chairs sometimes find it helpful to be given a brief background statement, summarising the aims and objectives of the party. If you are allowed to make such a statement you should attempt to set out:

- the issues you feel need to be resolved by the tribunal in order for you to win the case
- the evidence you will produce in order to prove each of these points
- any legal authorities you wish the tribunal to consider, eg statutes, cases, Codes of Practice.

Presenting your evidence

You then present your evidence. This stage is called 'evidence-in-chief'. This might consist of a mixture of documentary evidence and witnesses. You call your first witness to the stand. The tribunal clerk or member of the tribunal (or the Chair in Scotland) will usually swear in the witness, or the witness may choose to affirm that they promise to tell the truth (r8(4)).

The examination usually commences with the representative asking the witness to state their name and address and their position or previously held position in the organisation. Many people find it helpful to have prepared in advance a list of questions to put to their witnesses which:

- are relevant to the case
- the witness has actual knowledge of.

You may find it useful to rehearse with each of your witnesses in advance of the hearing the evidence which you are going to ask them to address. For example, you could let them know how their testimony fits in with the rest of the evidence and the kinds of questions you will ask them. However, you should not rehearse their answers or tell them what to say. In no circumstances should you encourage them to tell lies. Quite apart from the fact that they will be giving evidence under oath, they might well be discovered. The result will very probably be disastrous for your case, whatever its other strengths may be. Encourage them to say 'I don't know' or 'I can't answer that question', if they are asked a question to which they do not have a clear answer. This is preferable to inventing answers.

Your witnesses may be very nervous at the prospect of appearing before the tribunal. Try to reassure them that all you want from them is to tell the truth about matters which they know something about and nothing more. Try your best to make them feel relaxed about the appearance and reassure them that no-one will try and make them look foolish or silly. Most of all, however, make it absolutely clear that your case rests largely on the credibility of your witnesses. This means they must answer questions in a truthful, straightforward manner and try hard not to give evasive, 'clever' or sarcastic replies. They must not swear, enter into arguments, or, under any circumstances, lose their tempers. Point out that if during the cross-examination stage the other side asks questions which seemingly weaken your case, all is not necessarily lost; you will have the chance during re-examination to put things right. For example, re-examination will enable your witnesses to put their answers in the context in which the events actually occurred, thus repairing the damage that may have been done.

Encourage your witnesses to speak slowly and to speak to the Chair so that he or she can take a note of their evidence. If the Chair does not take notes, this may indicate that he or she considers the testimony to be irrelevant.

Remember that the purpose of calling a witness is for the witness to be seen and heard by the tribunal; it is not for the person conducting the questioning to make statements about what they think happened or whether the dismissal was fair or unfair.

Try to avoid asking leading questions, ie questions which invite a particular answer. Instead of asking the witness to confirm or deny a statement you have just made, try and get him or her to describe the events *in their own words*. This is likely to make a far greater impression on the tribunal. Sometimes, however, this approach may not be possible if the witness is noticeably nervous or inarticulate. Here the best course is to ask them to confirm or deny a statement you put to them.

Avoid calling evidence which could not have been known at the time the event complained of occurred, eg the dismissal. It is the fairness of the decision to dismiss at the time the decision was made that is being judged (although subsequent evidence may affect the amount of compensation the tribunal deems it just to award: **W Devis & Sons Ltd v Atkins** (see page 62).

Take notes of the testimony given by the witnesses. Without such notes the task of cross-examination, making a closing statement and mounting a subsequent appeal is made much more difficult. Supply your witnesses with pen and paper so that if they hear another witness making an inaccurate statement they can jot it down and show it to you. Unless this happens, people tend to forget very quickly.

When listening to the other side's witnesses giving their evidence-in-chief make a written note of:

- any inconsistencies you discover
- evidence they give which is at best hearsay and of which they have no personal or direct knowledge
- allegations they make which you will need to refute
- any mistakes or factual errors they make.

Occasionally witnesses ask to be allowed to read their testimony and sometimes this is allowed by tribunals. The other party should, however, ask to be given a copy so that they may more easily discover any discrepancies in the statement which they can then cross-examine.

Cross-examination

After your witness has given his or her evidence-in-chief, the other side is entitled to cross-examine them. The major importance of cross-examination is to elicit facts which will assist your case. To a large extent this depends upon having adequately prepared the case in advance so as to identify the precise points of contention and then establish what light this witness may be able to throw on this area. Therefore, confine your questioning to evidence given by the witness relevant to these points. It follows that you should ask questions on areas in which you have some degree of knowledge and should only reluctantly embark on a 'fishing expedition' into unknown waters.

The purpose of cross-examination should be:

- to expose inconsistencies in the evidence
- to correct confusing, misleading or untruthful evidence
- to put evidence into its correct context, eg by requiring a detailed answer
- to demonstrate conflicts of fact between the two sides
- to distinguish the witness' direct knowledge and experience from evidence which he or she has presented which is merely hearsay.

Do not waste time (and try the patience of the tribunal) by cross-examining on irrelevant or unimportant matters, or by asking a question repeatedly in the hope of getting a different answer from the one you have been given.

Cross-examination also involves drawing to the tribunal's attention at an early stage facts which you consider to be contentious. If you decide not to cross-examine a witness the tribunal may assume that you agree with everything they have said and may become annoyed if, when it is your turn to give evidence, it becomes clear that you do in fact disagree. If this does happen, the witness may have to be re-examined. Since witnesses are allowed to go home once they have given evidence, obvious problems can result.

A Chair will usually make extensive notes of the evidence, so wait until he or she has finished writing down the answer to the previous question before asking the next one. Remember also that as these notes exist it is usually futile to misrepresent what a witness said during his or her examination-in-chief.

It is normal practice in England and Wales for the witnesses of both sides to remain in the tribunal throughout the hearing. In Scotland the witnesses are requested to wait outside. However, you should consider asking the Chair to ask particular witnesses to leave the room where there are major disputes as to the facts. For example, there may be a difference of opinion as to precisely who said what to whom in the middle of a heated debate which preceded the decision to dismiss the applicant. Chairs are sometimes reluctant to do this but it does allow the party making the request greater scope for establishing discrepancies between the evidence given by the various witnesses.

You are not allowed to cross-examine your own witnesses in order to get them to change the evidence they have just given, but you may re-examine them in order to correct difficulties which may have arisen during the other side's cross-examination.

No case to answer

Once one of the parties has submitted all their evidence, the other party is then called upon to present theirs. If at this stage you feel that your opponent's case is so weak that even if everything they have presented to the tribunal is accepted as true, they must still in law lose the case, then you can attempt to persuade the tribunal that you have 'no case to answer'. The tribunal is unlikely to be convinced unless it is absolutely clear that the other party must lose, working on the old premise that there are usually two sides to most stories. If the tribunal does accept your argument the case is then immediately resolved in your favour. If your argument is not accepted then the case continues in the normal way by you calling your evidence.

Re-examination

After your witness has been cross-examined by the other side you have the opportunity to re-examine them in order to clarify any answer they may have given at that stage. However, you must not introduce entirely new evidence that was not referred to in the examination-in-chief or cross-examination. For example, a witness who in examination-in-chief was confident that he saw the applicant strike the supervisor, might have conceded in cross-examination that the lighting conditions were poor, that he was tired at the end of the day and that there were many other men around of the same colour, age and stature as the applicant. In re-examination you could ask the witness again if he was certain that it was the applicant who struck the man. So the purpose of this stage is to minimise damage that may have been imposed during the cross-examination. You can, therefore, try and place misleading remarks in their proper context and allow the witness to explain fully what he or she meant when they were forced by the other side to state simply 'yes' or 'no'.

After re-examination the Chair and tribunal members can, and frequently do, ask questions of the witness. These are often highly relevant and penetrating. If they raise new matters not previously looked at, then a witness may be brought back to give further evidence.

The closing statement

Both parties can make a closing statement. The final closing statement is usually made by the person on whom the burden of proof is placed, having been preceded by the other party, eg in a straightforward dismissal case where the fact that the applicant was dismissed was not disputed, the respondent employer would usually go last.

You should outline what you think are the important areas for the determination of the case in your favour and how the evidence shows that the arguments you advanced have been met. For example, you can point out:

- evidence which the other party has not challenged
- contradictions in the other party's case
- conflicting testimony in the other party's case
- that the applicant or respondent did, or did not, comply with relevant disciplinary procedures or Codes of Practice.

You should also mention here any legal matters which you wish the tribunal to consider, eg important past legal cases, sections of statutes or relevant Codes of Practice.

The decision

At the conclusion of the evidence the tribunal will retire to make its decision. Each member has one vote and the decision is made by majority vote (although in the vast majority of cases the decision is unanimous). If only two members heard the case then the Chair has a casting vote.

The usual practice is for the tribunal to retire for a short period of time and then come back and announce the decision verbally, together with the brief reasons for it. The formal written decision will then be posted to the parties several weeks later. Sometimes, however, the tribunal 'reserves' its decision, which means that it wishes to take time to consider the result of the case. Again, the written decision will be received by the parties some time later.

Whichever method is adopted, the tribunal is obliged to supply the parties with the written reasons, but these can be either in detailed or summary form (r9(3)). In either case you will be given the tribunal's basic findings of the facts which led it to arrive at the conclusions it did and what it believed the relevant law to be.

If the tribunal was unable to make up its mind on a particular point of fact over which the parties disagree, then it is entitled to decide the point in favour of the party who does not have the burden of proof placed upon their shoulders. For example, in **Morris v London Iron and Steel Ltd**, the tribunal could not decide whether the applicant had been dismissed or had resigned. It held that Mr Morris must lose the case as he had not discharged the burden of proof which was on him to show that he had been dismissed.

The decision is recorded in a document signed by the Chair which states whether the reasons are in full or summary form. In certain specified cases, however, the reasons must be in detailed form (r9(5)). These cases are as follows:

- equal pay, race and sex discrimination cases and those involving complaints relating to trade union membership and activities
- where one of the parties, either at the hearing or within 21 days of the date of which the document recording the summary reasons was sent to the parties, requests the detailed reasons
- where it appears to the tribunal itself that full reasons should be given, eg if the case will almost certainly be going to appeal, or if a complex point of law is involved.

If you think there is any prospect of your appealing to the Employment Appeal Tribunal you should ask for the full reasons, because a copy of them must be attached to your notice of appeal. You are given 21 days to request a copy of the full reasons.

The decision only becomes final when it has been signed by the

Chair and entered in the register at the COIT. Until then it is possible for the decision to be amended by the tribunal.

> 'This procedure is intended for the plain omission or the simple error which can be put right, and matters of that sort.'

Hanks v *Ace High Productions*

In *Lamont* v *Fry's Metals Ltd*, the tribunal changed its mind between making its oral decision and the decision being registered. It wrote to the parties, telling them that it wished to hear further argument on a particular matter concerning alleged redundancy. Following this further hearing the change of mind was confirmed. The Court of Appeal confirmed that industrial tribunals can alter their judgement at any time before registration.

Clerical errors or accidental slips or omissions can also be corrected by the Chair at any time (r9(9)). It is the date the decision is entered into the register that is important for the purposes of calculating how much time is allowed for requesting a review of the decision or appealing against it.

7 REMEDIES WHICH THE INDUSTRIAL TRIBUNAL CAN AWARD

Tribunals have three main powers. They can issue:

- an order for reinstatement or re-engagement (eg of an employee they have found to have been unfairly dismissed)
- an order that the employer pay compensation to the employee (eg because of an unlawful deduction taken from their wage packet). In the vast majority of cases this is the order that tribunals make
- a declaration of rights. Such declarations have considerable moral authority, but they cannot be directly enforced by any body or person. This means that if they are not complied with there is nothing that anybody can do about it.

Deciding upon the remedy

If the tribunal finds in favour of the applicant it will then have to make a decision as to the appropriate remedy. It might suggest that the parties agree among themselves as to the amount of compensation (usually to be preferred because it means that unemployment or supplementary benefit received by the applicant does not have to be paid back). In 1989–90, for example, in 38 per cent of successful unfair dismissal cases the remedy was left to be agreed between the parties (*Employment Gazette*, 1991 p304). Otherwise there will usually be a continuation of the hearing to decide upon the remedy or, possibly, a separately convened hearing to decide the matter if the tribunal had to retire to consider the case before making a decision. In unfair dismissal cases tribunals are obliged by s68 of the EPCA 1978 to explain to the applicant the different remedies that are available to the tribunal (reinstatement, re-engagement, compensation) and to ask which the applicant prefers. If the applicant seeks reinstatement or re-engagement the tribunal must then consider whether this is an appropriate remedy and whether it is 'reasonably practicable' to expect the employer to do this. It will also consider whether the applicant 'caused or contributed to some extent to his dismissal and whether it would be just to order his re-instatement' (EPCA 1978 s69(5)).

It is important to note at this point the case of **W Devis & Sons Ltd v Atkins**. This decision established the principle that the 'fairness' of a dismissal can only be determined on the facts known to the respondent employer at the time of the dismissal. Information subsequently obtained by the employer might be relevant for the purposes of reducing the amount of compensation to be paid to the applicant (indeed it might lead to an award of nil compensation), but not for determining the fairness of the dismissal.

In this case the employer dismissed a manager for failing to follow company instructions. After he left, the company allegedly discovered that he had been taking secret commissions from customers. The industrial tribunal refused to allow this evidence in relation to the fairness of the dismissal and this was upheld by the House of Lords on appeal.

Orders for re-employment

In dismissal cases the tribunal can 'order' that the employee be reinstated in the old job (ie taken back on the same terms and conditions of employment as before) or re-engaged in a different job with similar or different terms and conditions of employment. It rarely make such orders (there were only 59 in 1989–90 (*Employment Gazette*, 1991 p504)) but, in any event, the employee has a problem if the employer simply refuses to comply. This is because the tribunal has no direct power to enforce the 'order'. All it can do, upon the employee bringing the failure to comply to its notice, is to increase the compensation that would normally be payable to an employee in this situation by between 13 and 26 weeks' pay or, if the original reason for the dismissal was related to race or sex discrimination, by between 26 and 52 weeks' pay.

The reason for the inability to enforce such orders is usually said to be because this would be contrary to the general principle of law that no-one should be forced to become or remain a party to an employment contract against his or her will.

Compensation

In the vast majority of cases where the respondent loses the case, the tribunal orders the respondent to pay the compensation in a lump sum rather than in instalments. The average time before the lump sum is paid is four weeks. For those paid in instalments the average time for the first instalment to be paid is also about four weeks; for the final instalment it is about 12 weeks (*Employment Gazette*, 1990 p551).

Most respondent employers who have lost the case pay up without too many problems. In the event of default, however, the procedure which must be followed is cumbersome and time consuming. An originating application must be made to the county court nearest to where the losing party lives or carries on business. To this must be attached a written copy of the tribunal's decision accompanied by a sworn statement from the applicant which contains the amount of money outstanding. The application would usually be heard by the Registrar of the court who then decides whether to allow the respondent further time to pay or whether the money should be paid immediately. This means that the court will now enforce the decision as if it had made the order itself.

If the money remains unpaid, then the county court can send in the bailiffs to seize and sell the respondent's goods, order that the money be paid in instalments or indeed, invoke bankruptcy proceedings against the respondent. The court will then pay the relevant sum of money to the applicant. In Scotland the procedure is more simple and an application can be made to the Sheriff at his or her court who may then enforce the order.

You should note that in certain cases (mostly relating to unpaid redundancy payments and the basic award element of unfair dismissal compensation), direct application for payment can be made to the Department of Employment. These cases are where the respondent is insolvent or simply refuses to pay.

You can claim interest on compensation awards which the employer has failed to pay. As from 1 April 1990 interest at 15 per cent (subject to periodic review) is payable if the sum awarded remains unpaid 42 days after the tribunal's decision is recorded as having been sent to the parties concerned. Indeed, outstanding unpaid awards as at 1 April 1990 will also attract interest if they remain unpaid 42 days after that date. This new provision should tackle abuse and encourage prompter payment of awards in the future (Industrial Tribunals (Interest) Order 1990).

Is the Department of Employment entitled to some of my money?

The Department of Employment might well be entitled to some money. Given that part of the unfair dismissal compensation is to cover loss of earnings (if any), the Employment Protection (Recoupment of Unemployment Benefit and Supplementary Benefit) Regulations 1977 and 1980 provide that when the tribunal awards compensation it should indicate a 'prescribed element', ie the loss of earnings element of its award up to the date of the hearing. The Department of Employment is entitled to recover any unemployment or supplementary benefit it may have paid to the applicant from the prescribed element. Thus, the employer holds back from the applicant this part of the compensation and pays that amount to the Department. The balance should then be paid to the applicant. This procedure will be explained by the tribunal.

8 I LOST AND I WANT TO APPEAL

If, as either an applicant or a respondent you lost your case, you have two avenues available: review and appeal.

Review

In certain circumstances you can request the tribunal to review and to revoke and vary its decision. You *must* make the request either at the hearing or within 14 days of the entry of the decision in the register. Seeking a review is not a substitute for appealing, but a method of correcting mistakes of fact or law which you think the tribunal made and which came to light after the hearing. It is also, of course, considerably cheaper and more speedy than appealing (in 1990 the average length of time between receipt of a Notice of Appeal and the hearing of the appeal before the EAT was 16 months in England and Wales, and three months in Scotland).

Requests for a review are rarely made. They can only be made on the following grounds (r10(1)):

1　'The decision was wrongly made as a result of an error on the part of the tribunal staff'.
　　For example, a tribunal clerk failed to tell a witness that they were required in the hearing room.
2　'A party did not receive notice of the proceedings leading to the decision'.
　　For example, the respondent did not receive a copy of the originating application (although this is difficult to substantiate because once it is proved that the documentation was posted properly it is presumed that it was received by the person to whom it was sent).
3　'The decision was made in the absence of a party or person entitled to be heard'.
　　For example, where the employer was absent because he or she was given misleading information by the Department of Employment.

4 'New evidence has become available since the conclusion of the hearing ... provided that its existence could not have been reasonably known of or foreseen'.

In this case a full written statement of the new evidence must accompany the application for the review. It should be noted that the evidence must have become available *since* the hearing.

5 'The interests of justice require such a review'.

In this case, the tribunal would need very substantial grounds for allowing the review. The view is taken that, except in very unusual cases, it is in the interests of the general public that cases, once concluded, should be final. For example, where the tribunal may have simply overlooked some very important facts or refused to allow one of the parties to present evidence on a very important matter.

The procedure

The request is considered by the Chair of the tribunal that decided the case. The Chair can refuse the review 'if in his opinion it has no reasonable prospect of success' (r10(3)). If he or she does not refuse it then the original tribunal which decided the case will usually hear the application (unless it is no longer practicable to do so). If the tribunal grants the review it then reviews the decision and may then confirm, vary or revoke it. If it revokes it, the case is then re-heard before the same or a different tribunal (r10(4)).

You can request a review of the entire decision or of just one part of it, eg respondents can question the amount of compensation they have been ordered to pay to the applicant, or applicants may ask for a review if they feel thay have not been awarded enough compensation.

Appeal

You have a right to appeal to the Employment Appeal Tribunal (EAT) providing that you do so within 42 days of the entry of the decision on the register. Legal aid is available for appeals and, as with industrial tribunals, you have a right to be represented by anybody of your choice whether they are legally qualified or not. As has been previously noted, in 1989–90 the average delay between lodging a Notice of

Appeal and the hearing taking place was 16 months in England and Wales and three months in Scotland.

The appeal will be heard by a High Court judge who will act as the Chair, together with two lay colleagues. It is likely that one of these colleagues will be nominated by employer organisations and the other by trade unions. They are there because of their special knowledge of industrial relations; each of the three members has one vote. The EAT normally sits in London, Cardiff and Edinburgh.

The EAT hears appeals concerning points of law only (EPCA 1978 s136). Defining a point of law and distinguishing it from a point of fact is itself a very difficult task, but broadly speaking, the party who appeals must establish the following:

- that the tribunal misdirected itself in law, misunderstood it or misapplied the law, *or*
- that the tribunal misunderstood the facts or misapplied them, *or*
- that either the decision was perverse or that there was no evidence to justify the conclusion which was reached (ie no tribunal, properly directed in law, could have reached the particular decision that the tribunal reached).

A copy of the full written reasons of the tribunal decision must be served on the EAT by the appellant. Applications to the tribunal for the full written reasons must be made within 21 days of the date on which the document recording the summary reasons was sent to the parties (r9).

The EAT is reluctant to substitute its own opinion for that of the industrial tribunal and so it is not sufficient to show that the industrial tribunal decided to believe one witness rather than another, or even that the members of the EAT might have found in your favour had they been deciding your case at the industrial tribunal – you must demonstrate that the tribunal made an error in law.

If the appeal is based on an allegation that the tribunal took an erroneous view of the evidence or that it reached an unreasonable conclusion on the facts, then detailed particulars should be supplied and a preliminary hearing will be held to see if the full hearing should go ahead. During 1989–90 63 per cent of all such preliminary hearings were struck out at this stage (*Employment Gazette,* 1991 p307).

In this situation it is advisable to apply for the tribunal Chair's notes of evidence to be made available. These notes will usually be supplied on request, but in the event that they are not, the EAT itself can be asked to require them to be produced. In making its decision, the EAT balances the burden on the Chair, the reasons put forward by the appellant and the need to do justice between the parties (*Houston* v *Lightwater Farms Ltd*).

It is unusual for evidence to be given at the EAT hearing. EAT members hear legal argument rather than the evidence of live witnesses. It is extremely unusual for it to allow the introduction of new evidence, ie evidence not given at the tribunal hearing. This would only normally be allowed if:

- it was not available and could not have been obtained in time for the original hearing, *and*
- it would probably have had an important influence on the result of the case.

If the EAT allows the appeal, for example, finding that the tribunal erred in law in concluding that an employee was unfairly dismissed, it usually remits the case back to the original tribunal (or possibly a differently constituted tribunal) to re-hear the case either in total or in part. The only exception to this procedure is when the original decision is so clearly wrong that the EAT can substitute its own opinion and find, for example, that the dismissal was fair (*Morgan* v *Electrolux Ltd*).

The procedure

The procedural rules are contained in the Employment Appeal Tribunal Rules 1980 and in very detailed Practice Directions issued on 17.2.81 and 1.10.85. It is essential that anybody contemplating an appeal read both the Rules and the Directions. The Directions can be found in [1981] ICR at p287 and in [1985] ICR at p684, and can be looked up in Citizens' Advice Bureaux, law centres, academic law libraries, etc. They can also be found in *Butterworths Employment Law Handbook* (edited by P Wallington, 1990, (5th edition)) at p833.

For a detailed look at the practice and procedure at the EAT you should look at Chapter 11 of *Industrial Tribunal Practice*, (J Bowers, Longman, 1987), although it should be noted that this book is written mainly with the needs of lawyers in mind.

Further rights of appeal

You can ask the EAT to review its decision or can appeal on a question of law to the Court of Appeal (Court of Session in Scotland), but you may only do so with the permission of either the EAT or the Court of Appeal. It is also possible to take your point of law to the House of Lords but either that court or the Court of Appeal would need to certify that the point of law was one of 'general public importance'.

The EAT and the Court of Appeal both have power to refer cases to the Court of Justice of the European Communities for an authoritative interpretation of the Treaty of Rome 1957, or Directives which have been issued under it. They have both exercised this power in a number of cases concerned with equal pay and discrimination problems. For example, in 1990 the European Court of Justice upheld the principle that occupational pension schemes should apply the same retirement benefit to men as to women, and confirmed that Article 119 of the Treaty of Rome was of direct effect before UK courts. Hence no domestic legislation was required to implement it (**Barber** v **Guardian Royal Exchange Assurance Ltd**). As a result, almost all employers in the UK with company pension schemes have been required to review them and in many cases alter them.

9 THE PROCEDURE IN EQUAL VALUE CLAIMS

If a case involves a claim for equal pay the proceedings differ according to the basis of the claim. If it involves 'like work' (Equal Pay Act 1970 s1(2)(a)) or 'work rated as equivalent' (s1(2)(b)), the tribunal deals with the matter in the normal way so far as the procedure is concerned.

However, where an equal pay claim is based on what is now contained in the Equal Pay Act 1970 s1(2)(c), 'work . . . of equal value to that of a man in the same employment', a special procedure is used by the tribunals. The Industrial Tribunals (Rules of Procedure) Regulations 1985 specify, in sch 2, that at such a hearing it must first be determined if there are no reasonable grounds for the claim, eg that there is an important material difference between the job of the man and woman. For example, the respondent employer might argue that a job evaluation scheme which was non-discriminatory demonstrated that the woman's job was of less value than that of her comparator.

If the tribunal determines that the case should continue then it will appoint an independent expert, drawn from a list of people nominated by ACAS, to prepare a report. The expert will be supplied with a detailed brief specifying the precise questions he or she should investigate and report upon. If necessary, the expert can go back to the tribunal and ask it to use its powers to compel any person to supply written information or documents which that person has (although it may not order the disclosure of privileged information).

The expert will visit the applicant's workplace and conduct an investigation. He or she is required to take account of all the information supplied and all the representations made to them before drafting a summary which is sent to both parties seeking their observations. The expert then submits a report to the parties and to the tribunal. The tribunal is then reconvened to consider the contents of the report; this takes place usually about 10–12 months after the tribunal has adjourned the case.

Either side can argue that the report should not be admitted as evidence on the grounds that it is unsatisfactory, eg the expert failed to consider an important aspect of the claim, or arrived at a conclusion which could not reasonably be reached. If the report is accepted as evidence then each side can call one witness of their own to give expert evidence on the question which the expert was asked to consider. In practice this usually means that each side brings along their own expert to support or attempt to invalidate the independent expert's report. Both witnesses can be cross-examined and re-examined in the usual way.

The tribunal then decides whether or not the woman's work is of equal value to that of the man and whether, even if it is, there are any 'genuine material factors' which might justify a distinction in pay levels, for example, greater length of service or similar work but in different parts of the country.

In recent years there has been a substantial underlying increase in the number of equal pay applications dealt with by tribunals. It need hardly be pointed out, however, that few applicants who do not have the backing of their trade union or the Equal Opportunities Commission succeed in these complex equal value claims.

APPENDIX 1

Application to an Industrial Tribunal

Notes for Guidance

Before filling in this form please read:
- these GUIDANCE NOTES
- LEAFLET ITL1 which you were given with the form
- the correct BOOKLET for your type of case

Information: There are many things you can complain to a Tribunal about. LEAFLET ITL1 tells you what they are, which law (an Act of Parliament) covers your complaint, and which booklet you should get. Each of the BOOKLETS explains the law in simple terms. You can get the booklets free from any employment office, Jobcentre, or Unemployment Benefit Office. If you are in doubt, your Trade Union or a Citizens' Advice Bureau may be able to give you further advice or information.

Time limits: You must send in your application form so that it arrives at the Central Office of the Industrial Tribunals within the time limit. The time limit depends on which complaint you are making; for example, for unfair dismissal complaints it is three months beginning with the date of dismissal. So if you were dismissed on 10th January, the form must arrive by 9th April.

Qualifying periods: There are rules about how long you have to work for an employer before you can bring a case to a Tribunal. These rules are explained in the BOOKLETS.

If you are in any doubt about the time limits or qualifying periods, please contact your local employment office, Jobcentre, or Unemployment Benefit Office; or get in touch with the Advisory Conciliation and Arbitration Service (ACAS) - see the LEAFLET ITL1 for addresses and telephone numbers.

Representatives: You can present your own case at the Tribunal. If you want someone else to present your case, try to consult him or her before you complete your application form, but remember your form must arrive within the TIME LIMIT. If you name a representative, all future dealings will be with him or her and not with you. If you name a representative, you should ask him or her any questions you have about the progress of your case and when the Tribunal hearing will be.

If your complaint concerns EQUAL PAY or SEX DISCRIMINATION, you may wish to contact the Equal Opportunities Commission for advice or representation. If your complaint is about RACIAL DISCRIMINATION, you may wish to contact the Commission for Racial Equality for advice or representation.

Application to an Industrial Tribunal

Filling in the form

Help: Your Trade Union or local Citizens' Advice Bureau may be able to help you fill in the form if you have any problems, but make sure your form arrives within the TIME LIMIT.

Questions to answer: Try to complete all the boxes that apply in your case. You MUST answer the questions in boxes 1, 2, 4, 8 and 10.

Be clear: This form has to be photocopied, so please use black ink, or type your answers, and use CAPITAL LETTERS for names and addresses.

Box 1
Put here the type of complaint you want the Tribunal to decide (for example, unfair dismissal, redundancy payment, equal pay, etc.). A full list of types of complaint is given in the leaflet ITL1. If there is more than one complaint you want the Tribunal to decide, please say so. Give the details of your complaints in Box 10.

Box 2
Give your name and address and date of birth, and if possible a telephone number where the Tribunal or ACAS can contact you during the day about your application.

Box 4
Put here the name and address of the employer, person or body (the "respondent") you wish to complain about. In the second box, give also the place where you worked or applied for work, if different from that of the respondent you have named. (For example, complete both boxes if you have named a liquidator, the Secretary of State for Employment, or your employer's Head Office as the respondent).

Box 10
Give full details of your complaint. If there is not enough room on the form, continue on a separate sheet, and attach it to the form. Do NOT send any other documents or evidence in support of your complaint at this stage. Your answer may be used in an initial assessment of your case, so make it as complete and accurate as you can. (See **Help** above).

When you have finished:

- Sign and date the form
- Keep these Guidance Notes and a copy of your answers
- Send the form to:

ENGLAND AND WALES:

The Secretary of the Tribunals,
Central Office of the Industrial
  Tribunals
93 Ebury Bridge Road
London SW1W 8RE
Tel: 01-730 9161

SCOTLAND:

The Secretary of the Tribunals
Central Office of Industrial
  Tribunals (Scotland)
St Andrew House,
141 West Nile Street
Glasgow G1 2RU
Tel: 041-331 1601

Received at COIT	Case No.	Code
	Initials	ROIT

Application to an Industrial Tribunal

Please read the notes opposite before filling in this form.

1 Say what type of complaint(s) you want the tribunal to decide *(see note opposite)*.

2 Give your name and address etc. in CAPITALS *(see note opposite)*.

Mr/Mrs
Miss/Ms

Address

Telephone

Date of birth

3 Please give the name and address of your representative, if you have one.

Name

Address

Telephone

4 Give the name and address of the employer, person or body (the respondent) you are complaining about *(see note opposite)*.

Name

Address

Telephone

Give the place where you worked or applied for work, if different from above.

Name

Address

Telephone

5 Please say what job you did for the employer (or what job you applied for). If this does not apply, please say what your connection was with the employer.

IT 1 and IT 1(Scot) (Revised July 1987)

Please continue overleaf

INDUSTRIAL TRIBUNALS

6 Please give the number of normal basic hours you worked per week.

Hours [   ] per week

7 Basic wage / salary £ [   ] per [   ]

Average take home pay £ [   ] per [   ]

Other bonuses / benefits £ [   ] per [   ]

8 Please give the dates of your employment
(if applicable)

Began on [   ]

Ended on [   ]

9 If your complaint is **not** about dismissal, please give the date when the action you are complaining about took place (or the date when you first knew about it).

Date [   ]

10 Give the full details of your complaint *(see note opposite)*

11 Unfair dismissal claimants only (Please tick a box to show what you would want if you win your case).

[ ] Reinstatement: to carry on working in your old job as before

[ ] Re-engagement: to start another job, or a new contract, with your old employer

Orders for reinstatement or re-engagement normally include an award of compensation for loss of earnings.

[ ] Compensation only: to get an award of money

You can change your mind later. The Tribunal will take your preference into account, but will not be bound by it.

Signature: Date:

Printed in the UK for HMSO 12/87 Dd 804/097 C 2000 TP 19232

Industrial Tribunals

Case number:

Notice of Appearance by Respondent

1 Please give the following details

Mr ☐ Mrs ☐ Miss ☐ Ms ☐

Other title _____

(Or give the name of the company or organisation)

Name _____

Address _____

_____

_____

_____

Telephone _____

2 Do you intend to resist the application made by

_____

_____

YES ☐   NO ☐

3 Was the applicant dismissed?

YES ☐   NO ☐

If YES, what was the reason?

4 Are the dates of employment given by the applicant correct?

YES ☐   NO ☐

If NO, please give the correct dates

Began on _____

Ended on _____

5 If a representative is acting for you, please give his/her name and address (NOTE. *All further communications will be sent to him or her, not to you)*

Name _____

Address _____

_____

_____

_____

Telephone _____

Reference _____

6 Are the details given by the applicant about wages/salary or other payments or benefits correct?

YES ☐   NO ☐

If 'NO', or if details were not given, please give the correct details:

Basic wage/salary

£ _____ per _____

Average take home pay

£ _____ per _____

Other bonuses/benefits

£ _____ per _____

7 Maternity rights cases only

When the applicant's absence began did you have more than five employees?

YES ☐   NO ☐

Please continue overleaf ►

IT 3

INDUSTRIAL TRIBUNALS

8 If you answered 'YES' to question **2**, please give below sufficient details to show the grounds on which you intend to resist the application: *(continue on a separate sheet if there is not enough space for your answer)*

9	**10** Please send this form to:
Signed	The Assistant Secretary
	Regional Office of Industrial Tribunals
Date	London South
	93 Ebury Bridge Road
	LONDON SW1W 8RE

For official use

Date received _____   Initials _____

HQR.12.87

APPENDIX 2

Compensation limits (as from 1.4.91)

The following figures represent minimum and maximum awards. In practice, the compensation awarded might be reduced, eg if the tribunal considered the applicant had 'caused or contributed' to their own loss.

A 'week's pay' is the amount actually earned by the applicant, or a maximum of £198, whichever is less.

Unfair dismissal

	Limits	**Amount payable**
Basic award	£5,940 max	Depends on age, length of service and a 'week's pay'
Compensatory award	£10,000 max	Depends on actual loss
Additional award (for failing to comply with a tribunal order to re-employ)	£2,574 – 5,148 max	Between 13 and 26 weeks' pay
Additional award (where dismissal on racial or sexual grounds)	£5,148 – 10,296 max	Between 26 and 52 weeks' pay
Written reasons for dismissal		Two weeks actual pay

Unfair dismissal on grounds of trade union membership or activities where re-employment not sought

	Limits
Basic award	Min £2,650, max £5,940
Compensatory award	£10,000 max

Where re-employment sought but not granted

	Limits	**Amount payable**
Basic award	Min £2,650 max £5,940	
Compensatory award	£10,000 max	
Special award	Min £13,180 max £26,290	104 actual weeks' pay, subject to minimum

Where re-employment order not complied with

	Limits	**Amount payable**
Basic award	Min £2,650 max £5,940	
Compensatory award	£10,000 max	
Special award	Min £19,735 and no max	156 actual weeks' pay, subject to minimum

Equal pay

Limits	Amount payable
Arrears of pay for up to the last 2 years	Difference in pay between applicant and comparator

Guaranteed week payment

Limits	Amount payable
£13.65 per day, max of 5 days' pay in a 3 month period	Amount which should have been paid

Pay statements

Limits	Amount payable
Total of unnotified deductions in previous 13 weeks	Amount of unnotified deductions

Race discrimination

Limits
£10,000 max

Redundancy payment

Limits	Amount payable
£5,940 max	Depends on age, length of service and a 'week's pay'

Redundancy consultation

Limits	Amount payable
max 90 days' pay	Amount owing

Sex discrimination

Limits
£10,000 max

Suspension on medical grounds

Limits	Amount payable
max of 26 weeks' actual pay	Amount owing

Takeovers and mergers consultation

Limits	Amount payable
max of 2 weeks' pay	Amount owing

Time off work

	Limits	Amount payable
ante-natal care	No limit	Amount which should have been paid
public duties	No limit	
safety represen-tatives	No limit	Amount which should have been paid
redundancy	2 days of an actual week's pay	Amount which should have been paid
trade union duties and activities	No limit	

Trade unions

Limits	Amount payable

Exclusion or expulsion from a trade union:

Tribunal declaration followed by admission or re-admission	max £15,940	What the IT considers 'appropriate'
Tribunal declaration followed by a failure to admit or re-admit	min £2,650, max £26,236	Heard before the EAT

Unjustifiable discipline by trade union:

Tribunal declaration followed by trade union compliance	max £15,940	
Tribunal declaration followed by a failure to comply	min £2,650, max £15,940	
Victimisation short of dismissal in relation to TU membership or non-membership or participating in their activities	No limit	

Unfair recruitment

Limits

refusal of employment on union membership grounds	max £10,000

Wage deductions

Limits	Amount payable
No limit	The amount of unauthorised deductions

APPENDIX 3

Useful Addresses

ACAS (Head Office)
27 Wilton Street
London   SW1X 7AZ
Tel: 071 210 3000

(Regional offices are located at Birmingham, Bristol, Cardiff, Fleet, Glasgow, Leeds, Liverpool, London, Manchester, Newcastle-upon-Tyne, Nottingham)

Central Office of the Industrial Tribunals (England & Wales)
Southgate Street
Bury St Edmunds
Suffolk   IP33 2AQ
Tel: 0284 762300
Fax: 0284 766334

Central Office of the Industrial Tribunals (Scotland)
St Andrew House
141 West Nile Street
Glasgow   G1 2RU
Tel: 041 331 1601

Commissioner for the Rights of Trade Union Members
First Floor
Bank Chambers
2A Rylands Street
Warrington
Cheshire   WA1 1EN
Tel: 0925 415771

INDUSTRIAL TRIBUNALS

Commission for Racial Equality
Elliot House
10–12 Allington Street
London   SW1E 5EH
Tel: 071 828 7022

Employment Appeal Tribunal
4 St James Square
London   SW1Y 4JB
Tel: 071 210 3848

Equal Opportunities Commission
Overseas House
Quay Street
Manchester   M3 3HM
Tel: 061 833 9244

Free Representation Unit
13 Gray's Inn Square
London   WC1R 5JP
Tel: 071 831 0692

INDEX